MY SECRET DIARY

Giovanni Guareschi has also written

The Little World of Don Camillo

Don Camillo and His Flock

The House that Nino Built

Don Camillo's Dilemma

Don Camillo Takes the Devil by the Tail

MY SECRET DIARY

1943-1945

By GIOVANNI GUARESCHI

Translated from the Italian by Frances Frenaye

FARRAR, STRAUS AND CUDAHY / NEW YORK

CONTENTS

To My Comrades Who
Never Returned

He is reflecting that tonight in the Lager, *on the old camp-ground, no one is gazing up at the New Year's sky. He is thinking of the comrades that never returned, but that one day he will see again.*

On the tracks, a ghost train is silently running. This train has covered all the railroad lines of Germany, Poland, Russia and Yugoslavia, stopping at every concentration and internment camp along the way. It is an endless train, because it carries the souls of all those who died in imprisonment. Now it travels over the railroad lines of the Italian peninsula, halting wherever there is a former prisoner's soul to be gathered in. In fifty or sixty years, when all these souls have been collected, it will steam off on a sky-track, wherever God wills, and no one on earth will see it again.

He knows that one day the ghost train will stop at the station of his native town, and when he climbs aboard he will rediscover his lost comrades. And while he waits for the train to arrive, he is consoled by every passing year.

INSTRUCTIONS
FOR USE

This *Secret Diary* is so secret that it isn't a diary at all. I say this partly in order to correct the title of the book and partly in order to allay the misgivings of anyone whom it happens to antagonize.

It is not a diary in the sense of being a day-by-day account of what the writer thought and did, one of the usual compilations in which he regards himself as the center and fulcrum of the universe.

I did have the intention of compiling a diary of this kind, and for two years I jotted down everything I did or didn't do, everything I thought and saw, in-

cluding what I *should* have thought, even if I didn't
think it. As a result, I brought home with me three
bulky notebooks, containing enough material to fill a
volume of two thousand pages. As soon as I got there,
I put a new ribbon in the typewriter and set about
deciphering and amplifying my notes. Out of the two
years I did not skip a single day.

It was a tiresome and feverish job but, at the end,
my diary was complete. I reread it attentively,
polished it up and tried to give it a good tempo. Then
I had it retyped and, after all this was done, I put it
away with the intention of never looking at it again.
This, I believe, is one of the wisest acts of my whole
career as a writer.

* * *

It came about that, like millions and millions of
others, I was involved in the most recent of the messes
into which our unfortunate world has got itself. I
don't remember exactly how it went. Almost every
participant in a war has so much to do in the small
sector allotted to him that he cannot keep himself informed of the all-over picture. He doesn't know
whether he's winning or losing and, even at the end,
whether he has won or lost the war.

There were enemies who turned out to be allies,
and allies that became enemies. And to the war
among nations there was added the political and civil
war, which set parents against children, husbands
against wives, north against south and east against
west. An objective historian can, in strict honesty,

only write: "In a world of madmen, the mad were conquered by the mad." Because if the one side was madder than the other, the other was also madder than the one.

Like millions of others, better and worse than myself, I was drawn into this war. As an Italian, I found myself an ally of the Germans at the start and at the end their prisoner. In 1943 the Anglo-Americans bombed my house; in 1945 they freed me from prison and gave me cans of soup and condensed milk. As far as I am concerned, that is the whole story. I had no more influence than a nutshell tossed about on the ocean, and I emerged without ribbons or medals on my chest. I emerged as a victor, however, because I came through the cataclysm without hatred in my soul and I made the discovery of a precious friend, myself.

As for the exact course of my personal story, it was this. One day in September of 1943, I found myself, along with a group of other officers, in an internment camp in Poland. Subsequently I changed camps several times, but the story remained essentially the same. It's no use going into all the details, because anyone who wasn't a prisoner in this last war or the one before it will probably be a prisoner in the next. If he has not had the experience himself, then a father has had it before him or a son will have it after, or else he has heard about it from a brother or a friend.

For present purposes, the only thing of interest is

that, even in prison, I remained a stubborn native of the province of Emilia, of the lower reaches of the Po valley; I gritted my teeth and said to myself: "I won't die, even if they kill me!" And I didn't die, either, probably only because they didn't kill me, but at any rate I didn't die. I stayed alive in spirit as well as in body, and kept right on working. I wrote not only notes for my diary, but also a number of things for everyday camp use.

Indeed, I spent a good part of my time going from hut to hut and reading aloud the sort of thing of which the present book will furnish examples. Pieces which were intended at the time only for camp consumption and not at all for publication in the world outside the *Lager.* And yet, now that years have gone by, these pieces are the only ones that seem to me to have some validity. Having locked up my diary, I searched among the greasy, thumb-marked sheets of my camp writings and made up this "secret" collection.

As I have said before, it is a diary so secret as not to be a diary at all. Yet, in many ways, it seems to me to give a better picture of those days, and their thoughts and sorrows than my huge original compendium. Nothing else, I repeat, is valid or deserving of publication. This material is what you might call "authorized." I thought it out and wrote it in the *Lager;* most of it I read aloud a dozen or more times, and it won general approval. The only part of this book which has not been passed upon by my camp

comrades is the Epilogue, which I published in a
weekly paper, after our return home. The rest has
been cleared for transmission.

*   *   *

To my camp comrades I am No. 6865, and I count
as only one man. Among those melancholy wastes,
every one shed his protective covering and all other
external appurtenances; being left naked, he showed
himself for what he really was. The big name that
so-and-so had in the outside world, or his high rank
in the army, didn't matter; every one counted only as
much as he was intrinsically worth. Every one of us
was a single unit, and he was judged solely by performance.

Our feet were planted solidly on the ground. For
almost two years we lived in a true democracy, made
up of men who were honest and true. Now many of
us play an important part in the public and private
life of a democracy that is not a democracy, and in
which honesty is notably lacking. Perhaps our old
comrades can never again be the honest fellows they
once were, because environment makes the man. It is
for their benefit that I am publishing this book, in
order to give them a whiff of the fresh air we used to
breathe together.

*   *   *

We didn't live like brutes; we didn't shut ourselves
up in our selfishness. Hunger, dirt, cold, illness, the
desperate longing for our homes and families and the
dark sorrow we felt for the misfortunes of our coun-

try were not sufficient to dampen our spirits. We never forgot that we were civilized men, heirs to a past and possessors of a future.

*   *   *

We were loaded onto freight cars and then unloaded from them, stripped of most of our belongings and thrown into the bug-ridden filth of the *Lager*. Buried in communal graves around us were the bodies of thousands of our predecessors.

Soon the outside world forgot. The International Red Cross could do nothing for us, because its charter contained no provisions for our status of "military internees." Of the two opposing Italian military leaders, both of them equally damaging to their country, who might have raised a voice on our behalf, one[1] was our declared political enemy, while the other[2] chose to ignore us, because politics took all his time.

We didn't want material help; all we needed was a word of encouragement. But we were spoken of either disparagingly or not at all. We built radios which were miracles of ingeniousness, tributes to the inventive power Italians can summon up under adversity. Over these we heard millions of words in every language, but never a word in our own tongue, broadcast for us to hear. In the south of Italy, political mummies palavered, while in the north, striplings, poisoned by politics, tried to kill one another.

---

1 Graziani.
2 Badoglio.

Every now and then some representative of our country did talk to us from outside the barbed-wire enclosure. It was always to say the same thing: that the way of duty and honor was not to embrace voluntary imprisonment, but to go home, where thousands of our fellow-citizens, underground or in the Allied camp, were waiting for us to come shoot them.

We were worse than abandoned, and yet we did not turn into brutes. Out of nothing we rebuilt our civilization. We organized spot news talks, lectures, church services, university courses, plays, concerts, art exhibitions, sports, crafts, a library, regional assemblies, a radio listening center, a commodity exchange, want ad publication and enterprises of both manufacturing and trade.

As I have said, every one was suddenly laid bare, leaving his rank and reputation, however well or ill deserved, outside. He was left with nothing but his own interior resources, rich or meager, as the case might be, and gave what he had it in him to give. In this new world, every one was a single unit, judged by his intrinsic worth.

In the *Lager* life was always the same: the same stretches of sand, the same huts, the same bleakness. But there was everything a civilized man needed in order to live in a civilized way. Everything, even the latest song hit, which was hummed and whistled all over the lot. It was a civilized song, because both words and music faithfully mirrored the best feelings of us all.

We did not live like brutes; out of nothing we built our own Democratic City. If now, many ex-internees are shocked by the spectacle of everyday life and hold themselves aloof, it is because the image of Democracy which they came to cherish in imprisonment was so different from the false version they see around them, the usual sea of intrigue, with pirates, old and new, at the helm of the pirate crafts of yore. These disappointed men are doubtless the most honest among us. To them, as well as to those who have adjusted and adapted themselves, I address these pages.

The voice of No. 6865 is speaking, the same voice, coming out from under the same handlebar mustache. Nothing has been added. I abandoned my original diary, because I had no right to say things about the *Lager* to which my *Lager* companions had not given the stamp of their approval. I am the same democrat now as I was then. I haven't my fleas and lice and bedbugs, or the rats that used to run over my face; I have a listless appetite instead of a devouring hunger, and in my pocket are all the cigarettes I care to smoke. But I am the same democrat I was before, and no word which my comrades have not approved shall be printed here, and I mean my dead comrades as well as my living ones. For in a true Democracy, we must take account of the dead.

As for the others, those who didn't share our humble adventure, I don't know what effect these pages will have upon them. Perhaps they will be bored. But then, in those days, I was bored, too. Perhaps the idea

of the book, at least, may amuse them, the idea of a
humorist's account of his prison. Anyhow, here it is,
ready for my twenty-three faithful readers. If it's not
all right, then next time I'm interned, I'll try to do
better.

1943

Letter to My Descendant: 1

Dearly beloved Descendant:

After an experience as harrowing as the one it has just lived through, the human race is hellbent on keeping out of all future wars. The present scourge, then, is definitely the last of its kind to afflict us.

Thus you too, beloved descendant, may some day find in your mailbox a summons to appear at such-and-such an army barracks, where you will be equipped with tools enabling you to do unto your neighbor just as much harm as you can do unto yourself. And eventually, after a long train of vicissitudes, you may wind up, like your unfortunate forefather, in an internment camp.

I can't definitely inform you whether the guard on the watchtower above you will be English, Russian, French, German or Italian. But no matter what his nationality, he'll make an effort to place a bullet in your back if you try to fly the coop. That's all you have coming to you. And that is why there is some point to my explaining, on the basis of my own experience, how and why you may land behind a barbed-wire fence.

*   *   *

One morning, as I stood in my trim artillery lieutenant's uniform, on the barracks parade ground, the bugle called me to attention and something truly extraordinary happened: my heels snapped together with a resounding click.

In order to appreciate the import of this event, we must look back at the long, sad story of my so-called "unsoldierly attitude."

One dreary November day, I traveled to the foggiest city of Italy and managed, with some difficulty, to locate the barracks where I was supposed to report.

There an authoritative-looking individual told me:

"Beginning tomorrow, you'll be in charge of the Sixth Anti-Aircraft Battery, in process of formation."

I assured him that as a field artillery man, I hadn't even a bowing acquaintance with anti-aircraft weapons.

"Doesn't matter," he answered brusquely, nodding at a noncommissioned officer who proceeded to load me with notebooks and papers. He himself handed me an ordinary pen and said gravely:

"Remember these supplies have got to last you a whole month. Mind you don't bother me with requests for extras!"

As he saw me through the door, he cordially advised me to lose no time setting up a ledger and roll call.

"Those are basic," he assured me.

I thanked him for his advice and asked where I was to find my station.

"In the company office, of course. Every unit has one."

"And where is it, if you please?"

"You Reserve shavetails will drive me crazy!" he shouted. "How can you ask? Wander around and question everyone you meet, and you'll find a place to make into a company office."

"But I—"

"Use your head!" he yelled, slamming the door behind me.

The pen fell on the floor and I inadvertently stepped on it.

"Goodbye to my monthly supplies," I said, giving it a melancholy salute.

*   *   *

I wandered all over the barracks, still staggering under the load of my notebooks and papers, but everyone I questioned about an empty spot suitable for a company office simply shrugged his shoulders in reply. All in vain I slipped twenty liras to the watchman at the supply depot, who was said to be a Very Important Person. And equally in vain I explained to the sergeant in charge of Upkeep and Repairs that the general situation was critical and a new anti-aircraft battery might save the day, but that this battery's formation depended on the setting up of a company office. From purely patriotic motives, he said, he was ready to plaster and paint any place I succeeded in finding. Only I had to find it.

After much wandering, I came upon a young fellow who took it upon himself to claim allegiance to my future anti-aircraft battery and to offer his services as company clerk. I enrolled him on the spot, handed over my load of notebooks and papers, and made him a member of my searching party. Eventually, however, I realized that my office staff couldn't be a mobile affair. With my new recruit in tow, I decided to leave the barracks behind me.

"Our office is *here*," I announced, when we came to the furnished room I had rented earlier in the day. "Pick yourself up a subordinate who can, in his turn, take on all the personnel you need, and go quietly to work. I'm moving to a hotel." And just to make things easier for him, I signed some seventy-five passes.

The goings and comings of large numbers of enlisted men led people to draw entirely mistaken conclusions, and my rooming house proceeded to lose its good name. Aside from this, everything went swimmingly for just as long a time as I needed to complete my search within the precincts of the barracks. But the episode was branded "unsoldierly," and I became an object of suspicion.

There were other little episodes of the same kind, which further undermined my reputation, but the last straw was the "coffee crime."

One morning my sixty men informed me that, thanks to some sort of confusion in the kitchen, none of them had had a drop of coffee to drink. My only answer was to line them up, march them out of the barracks, divide them among the four nearest cafés and treat them, out of my own pocket, to what they needed so badly.

The dim view that my superiors took of this excursion gave rise to the legend of my "unsoldierly attitude" and indeed damaged me so far that I was relieved of the command of the now definitely formed anti-aircraft battery.

If I had been sent to the front, I might have had a chance to see some of the famous anti-aircraft weapons. But it was my fate to remain in the rear. As an anti-aircraft man I am, even today, sincerely sorry. But at the time, my attention was distracted by another bit of trouble, connected with heel-clicking.

*　　　*　　　*

Do colonels dream?

Yes, colonels do dream, just like everyday human beings and reserve officers. Indeed, their dreams are almost identically the same. Army regulations are not concerned with dreams, and many an old-time colonel dreams about angels. Angels with pale blue wings and golden hair, that glide down to earth as gently as those which people the dreams of poets and young girls. Only when such angels land at a colonel's feet, they draw themselves to attention with a sharp click of their heels.

Now if any creature, mortal or immortal, in this world or the next, is entitled to go barefoot, surely it is an angel. But colonels are so dead set on heel-clicking that the angels of their dreams never fail to put on a

stout pair of army boots, and if the colonels belong to
the cavalry the boots have spurs attached.

Well then, beloved descendant, since your gentle forefather knew how deeply colonels care for clicking heels
and he was in daily contact with an old colonel, he
couldn't very well overlook this little detail. Indeed,
clicking heels were, at this time, one of my chief con-
cerns. I knew that only a succession of successful clicks
could destroy the myth of my "unsoldierly attitude."
But fate was against me. I tried three different pairs of
boots and six pairs of spurs, I sought out the expert advice of a blacksmith and a chiropodist, I took private les-
sons from a retired cavalry sergeant, I made a plaster
model of my feet and studied their contour, I practiced
conscientiously in front of a mirror . . . but when it
came to the real thing, my heels were like jellied con-
sommé and my spurs like pats of butter.

Plunk! And every plunk brought an expression of
acute pain to the colonel's face.

The severest ordeal, and one which I had to face twice
a day, was in the mess hall, where the colonel was
flanked by a group of high-ranking officers. As soon as
they saw me enter the hall, there was a moment of complete silence. Every ear pricked up, and every eye was
upon me. I raised my arm in the prescribed salute and
desperately drew my heels together.

Plunk! It was like a butter pat falling into a pile of
flour. The colonel sorrowfully shook his head and all
those present returned to their food. Over every single

inclined head I saw a sort of comic-book legend, in letters of fire, reading: "Unsoldierly!"

Finally I made a deal with a heel-clicking regular army lieutenant, who sat near the door. When I came in and saluted, he was to click his heels under the table. Operation Dubbing, you might have called it, but I tried it twice and no more. The first time, the click came a whole minute after I had come to attention, the second while I was still walking into the room. And so I went back to my *plunks,* and the colonel continued to look as pained as if I had stuck a pin into his heart. *Plunk! Plunk!* How many times did I hear that miserable sound?

One autumn morning, when I was standing in line in the barracks courtyard, and the bugle called me to attention, something miraculous happened. My heels came together with a resounding click. *Tac!*

"At last!" I exclaimed triumphantly.

Then I looked down at my feet and saw the reason why. All my cockiness faded away. I was wearing not my regulation boots, but a pair of wooden shoes whose soles were three inches above the ground. I was a prisoner of war.

*   *   *

That, dear descendant, is the whole story. Next time I'll tell you how I came to be in the great central yard of a *Polish* barracks. Meanwhile, give your mother, grandmother and sister my love; be a good boy at school and learn to count up to 6865. Which is the number of your devoted

Father.

The Black Madonna

September 20

I feel as if I were walking through the streets of a city devastated by the plague. The few people to be seen walk as hurriedly as if someone were following them and cast hasty glances at the ten prisoners of war, preceded by a Gestapo captain and with a suspicous *Dolmetscher* (interpreter) bringing up the rear. No matter how fleeting these glances, there is an eloquence in their eyes which only the interpreter is powerless to understand.

Before 1939, Czestochowa was a city of 180,000 inhabitants; a few days after the entrance of the Germans 50,000 of these were gone, transferred to some other locality, in this world or the next. It seemed as if houses, as well as men, had been deported, taken away from the vast area of wide, empty streets and squares. The surviving buildings were all sad in appearance, as if they had souls and their outward aspect reflected the tragedy which had haunted them for the last four years.

The air was heavy with suspicion; eyes peered out between half-closed shutters, shops were locked and the windows of the few still open displayed the canned and boxed products in which impoverishment tries to conceal itself: dried-egg mixes, fruit and vegetable extracts, soap powder and little bags of desiccated herbs. Every now and then there was a glass jar filled with licorice sticks or bright-colored candies, to convince children that something had been spared by the war.

PATRIA BAR . . . the Italian word on the sign over-hanging the entrance to a deserted café gave the heart a twinge like that provoked by the sight, among a foreign crowd, of one familiar face.

The streets were swept with wind which howled in my empty head. I felt like a desperate character who puts on his last good suit and goes to stroll on the main street, among the crowd of rich men and beautiful women, stopping to stare at jewelers' windows and to ask for somebody by name in the best café, knowing all the while that this world is no longer his and he has no right to be walking in it. For the moment I had forgotten, but I was sure that as soon as the gate closed behind me I should remember that for a full month I had been hungry.

*   *   *

The Sanctuary is on top of a hill and as soon as we started up the broad approach, the Gestapo captain stopped and spoke to the interpreter, who immediately translated his words for our benefit.

"The captain says the hill you see is more than four hundred feet above sea level."

This was the only thing he found worthy of note. After all, altitude is a factual, mathematical sort of thing, as distinct from artistic and historical properties. A very German point of view.

At the entrance to the Sanctuary we were met by a German-speaking guide. One of the prisoners served as his translator.

The Sanctuary is an agglomeration of buildings

around a very high bell tower. Originally it was a monastery belonging to the Order of St. Anthony Abbot, later incorporated with that of the Dominicans. After the year 1200, when the monastery acquired possession of the famous St. Luke Madonna, it was the goal of many pilgrimages, and the chapel grew into the size and importance of a consecrated basilica.

Priors and Polish lords made successive additions to the physical plant, and thus it became a sort of architectural encyclopedia. Even the lofty, black marble bell tower seems to have been designed by an architect who drew spire after spire and said after every one: "Let's add something more. We have a long way to go before we touch the feet of St. Peter!"

In short, the effect is that of a jumble, with all around it the world's largest-scale Stations of the Cross, composed of fourteen twice-lifesize, sculptured figures, on pedestals fifty yards one from another. Inside, there is such a quantity of marble, both genuine and fake, that when the visitor steps out onto the black and white pebbles of the open square in front, he is tempted to trample them with his heels in order to find out whether they are made of painted wood or real stone.

In certain places, the Sanctuary has something of a citadel about it. High black boots are visible below the white robes of the monks, giving them a disguised soldier's air. (The same thing can be said of many Polish men.) It must, indeed, be a mighty stronghold, in order to have withstood the attacks of Swedes, Hussites, Russians and Saxons. In 1709, the Swedes stormed and took

its impregnable heights, which were manned by only
two hundred and twenty monkish and lay defenders.
Twelve thousand Swedes were not sufficient, and it took
eighteen thousand to make it fall. The guide pointed
out cannon balls which were imbedded in the walls at
this time.

*   *   *

Everywhere, in the square, on the steps, the railings,
the mural decorations and the spires, there are the palm
tree with two rampant lions and the raven carrying a
piece of bread in his beak, which pertain to the legend
of St. Anthony in the desert. Every day the raven
brought him half a loaf of bread and, when St. Anthony
went to visit him, once a year, a whole one. And when
the saint died two lions dug his grave with their claws.

In a low voice the guide added a postscript to his
story. "Originally the bird was an eagle. When the Russians came along, they substituted for it a raven. Then
came the Germans, and took away the bread."

*   *   *

From the square there is a view over the whole city
and the woods stretching all the way to the horizon,
which once belonged to the monastery.

"During the pilgrimages made to honor the feast day
of the Black Madonna, there are arrangements in the
great courtyard for the confessions and communions of
fifty thousand persons a day. And at the altar up there,
behind a movable glass door, Mass is said for the hundreds of thousands clustered at the foot of the hill. Naturally, there are loudspeakers . . ."

The guide continued his humdrum spiel, calling attention to the cost of all these installations and the name of the contractor who had built them. I looked down at the foot of the hill, where hundreds of thousands of Poles are wont to gather. The only human soul was a scurrying woman in high boots, whose presence only served to set off the solitude and despair of the empty space all around her.

*   *   *

It was time to attend the daily ceremony held at the basilica.

The Black Madonna of Czestochowa is said to be the earliest known portrait of the Blessed Virgin, painted from life by St. Luke on a fragment of the board over which She wept during the Crucifixion. This piece of wood has a most interesting story, having stayed for 320 years in Jerusalem, 400 in Constantinople, 400 in Hungary and ever since 770 years ago here at Czestochowa. In 1430 it was stolen and mutilated by Hussites from Bohemia (it is riddled with Tartar bulletholes as well). In 1717 it was consecrated by Pope Clement X, and we see it today enshrined in a chapel whose display of gold, silver and precious stones is so rich as to be almost alarming, for after a certain point wealth is divorced from reality and becomes inadmissible. The image is lodged in a niche above the altar, covered by a massive, solid gold block, weighing 1,600 pounds, which can be raised and lowered, like a curtain, before it. Every afternoon, at a quarter to five, there is a brief ceremony, during which the image is exposed to the public view, to the accompaniment of a hymn composed by Perosi when he was a guest of the monastery in 1909.

(Perosi's is not the only Italian name. A sculptor called Fontana worked from 1690 to 1726 on one of the altars of the basilica, which he ornamented with an immense statuary group, wreathed in clouds of Florentine *tufo,* weighing at least ten tons each, which overhang the scene as oppressively as if from one moment to the next they might crumble, and rain down a shower of stone.)

*   *   *

Entering the basilica, we found ourselves among a crowd of women and children gathered in front of a fairytale altar, gleaming with jewels and lights, while an organ played in the background. After a month in surroundings where everything oozed filth and despair, where every spoken word was a cry and every order a threat . . . to be suddenly plunged into this atmosphere of calm, this glitter of gold, this warm flow of music! . . .

I paused at the threshold, then stepped forward, feeling suddenly as buoyant as if I had shed my rag-covered body at the door. The gold block in front of the niche slowly rose, and the miraculous image—pitch-black against the gleaming gold—was by virtue of the very contrast utterly mysterious and fascinating.

From the crowd there rose a song which seemed to express the whole soul of Poland, to voice the dignified sorrow of a people accustomed for centuries to oppression and resurrection.

When the gold block was lowered, there was a fanfare

of trumpets whose notes were filled with a desperate and deeply disturbing passion.

"The trumpeters are playing out of tune because some of the best of them are absent," explained the guide.

So that was it: those notes of desperate passion were simply out of tune. Very well, then. But I, for one, didn't believe it. Everything in Poland, every gesture and intonation, speaks of passion.

* * *

Dusk fell over the dark blue-green woods around Czestochowa. From the square in front of the Sanctuary we could see a pale moon preparing for the evening spectacle and, on the left, the huge Nordkaserne, with the towers set at intervals around its barbed-wire fencing.

"The carillon in the bell tower is one of the best in the world," the guide told us.

"And why doesn't it ever ring?"

"Ever since the first day of the German occupation, all the bells have been silent," he said under his breath. "They won't ring again until Poland is free."

As we prisoners filed back down to the city, I thought of the four years that the bells had been mute. Should I hear the bells of Poland peal again?

* * *

October 31

Many of the captured Russian coats which the Germans have distributed to us have a patch on the chest or back, a little, round patch covering the hole where a bullet went in and a soul went out. My coat has such a patch, just over the heart. It is made of stout cloth and carefully sewn, yet a breath of cold air penetrates the patch, even when there is no wind and a warm sun. And my heart aches, when it is pierced by this icy needle.

Second Letter

Dearly beloved Descendant:

In my first letter I told you how, one fine morning, I found myself in the courtyard of the Nordkaserne at Czestochowa. Now I shall tell you how I got there.

* * *

It was the evening of September 8, 1943, when suddenly the radio broadcasted that it was all over. This was so true that the next morning I woke up in the same barracks, but under the watchful eye of sentries quite different from those that had gone before, different in regard to uniforms, weapons and, alas, nationality as well. The general appearance of the barracks had also undergone a change, thanks to a certain number of artillery pieces, awkwardly inserted among the architectural glories of the façade. In other words, the Germans had taken over.

"And what about the heroic, last-ditch defense?" you may ask.

Just let me tell you one story, my dear fellow, the most dramatic of the lot.

We were under siege, and waiting from one moment to the next for the beginning of the attack. I was in command of twenty-five men, at the truck entrance. The corporal whom I had sent to the supply depot came back and I asked him:

"How many hand grenades did you get us?"

"No hand grenades," he answered. "The major told me that without a regular requisition he can't give out so much as a pin. He doesn't want to get into hot water."

"All right," I said. "What about cartridges for our rifles? How many have we on hand?"

"One round per man."

"Never mind!" I shouted. "We'll have to be sparing with our shots. Aim at the whites of their eyes!"

"How are we to do that?" one of the soldiers objected. "They'll be in tanks."

"Then aim at the tanks! What else can I say?"

*   *   *

So much for history. For the purposes of a play-by-play account, let us admit that it was all over, but that our troubles had just begun. Toward noon, the rank and file were transferred to the outskirts of the city, while the officers were taken to the "Gastric Ulcer," otherwise known as the "Garrison Mess." It was a kind thought, when you come down to it, to invite us to lunch. Unfortunately, a big German tank had swept through the mess hall before us, and the follow-up infantry had streamed through the kitchen. So we found it advisable to take refuge, very sleepily, in the clubrooms on the second floor.

That night we managed as best we could. The colonel stretched out on the billiard table, alongside the major. Poor colonel! I remember that he snored in the same key as the march from *Tannhäuser,* and this nocturnal tribute to the musical genius of our great ex-ally was both gallant and pregnant with meaning.

I slept on the grand piano, and dreamed all night long of Heine's poem about the Two Grenadiers.

The next day, after a lively discussion with an S.S. officer, we were moved to the Citadel.

"Citadel?" you may ask. "What's that?"

"Well, just imagine that an architect of times gone by drew up the plan of a fortified place intended to lodge soldiers and provide storage for their weapons as well. He took pains to make the whole thing highly functional and common-sensical. But then, imagine this: the architect had to go away and in his absence his pet dog, Flick, chewed the blueprint to pieces. And the chambermaid, in order to cover up the disaster, picked up the pieces and glued them together in strictly haphazard fashion. The architect arrived upon the scene, took in at a glance the gravity of what had happened, but simply shrugged his shoulders and said: 'It doesn't really matter!' He sent the blueprint to the war department, where it was enthusiastically approved and forwarded to the contractors, who proceeded to put it into execution.

This is a Citadel. And now you can see why, in the course of your tour of a Citadel, or for that matter of any ordinary military installation, you may come across a room in the shape of a triangular pyramid with the door at the summit, a latrine with the toilet seat stuck onto the ceiling, a balcony opening onto a long hall, a nine-foot door on the third floor connecting with empty space, or a waterpipe running into a chimney.

In August, 1932, in the Citadel of P., I met a strangely accoutered soldier with a long, white beard.

"In what year were you called to do your military service?" I asked him.

"1899," he told me.

"And are you still on duty?"

"No, sir," he replied. "I got my discharge in 1904, but I couldn't find the way out . . ."

The Citadel of A. was of this same kind, but luckily, after only a few days had gone by, they took us to a *Lager,* where we were considerably better off. Yes, dear Descendant, God preserve you from citadels! For one thing, their walls are horribly hortatory. There isn't an inch of space that doesn't bear some such message as: NOTHING VENTURED, NOTHING GAINED! BELIEVE, OBEY, FIGHT! MY COUNTRY, RIGHT OR WRONG! EXCELSIOR!

In one picturesque spot, divided into small compartments, I read in huge letters: RUN! Considering the urgency of the emergency, this was really too much to ask.

In the Citadel of A. I had occasion to notice various interesting things. For instance, I made my first acquaintance with a German horse. He was a dignified, warlike animal; the look in his eye and his proud demeanor showed that he was conscious of the gravity of the times and the significance of his allotted task, which was no less than the construction of a new pan-European equine society.

He was attached by a formidable complex of harness to a very special kind of small carriage made of iron and cast iron. This carriage was equipped with so many wheels, levers, pedals, hand- and foot-brakes, that one might have supposed it had an accelerator, clutch and gearshift as well. The remarkable thing about the harness was that every one of the holes in the multitude of straps was labeled with a conspicuous, individual number. It looked like a triumphant attempt to mechanize the humble horse. The girth was pulled so tight that his waist was as wasplike as that of any ballet dancer, whereas the breeching was several inches too long and hung slackly under the tail. Apparently German regulations required that this particular type of horse should have its girth fastened at hole number 27, and the breeching at number 12. The good creature was not annoyed by this state of affairs, but rather looked slightly ashamed of the fact that his mother had not shaped him in such a way as to fit the official pattern. If the God of horses had said to him: "Ask, and it shall be given," I am quite sure that he would have asked for his waist to be reduced in size and his tail, together with the hindquarters, to be lowered a good six inches.

*   *   *

How long did I stay in the Citadel of A.? It doesn't in the least matter. The point is that one day I came out and was put on the train which was to carry us north of the Alps. It was then that I had a last glimpse of my old bicycle.

I had managed to take my bicycle to the "Gastric Ulcer" and then to the Citadel. But I couldn't get it loaded on the truck which carried us to the station. There was considerable discussion until I was silenced by the conclusive remark:

"We have orders to intern Italian officers, not Italian bicycles."

And so, very sadly, I left it leaning up against a wall, under a great printed slogan: WIN THE WAR OR BUST!

Dear Descendant, that is all for today. Give my love to your mother, grandmother and sister Carlottina. Be a good boy, and some day you too will have a number, such as 6865, which is that of your devoted

Father.

Lily Marlene

November 4

In the pages of the German novelist Wiechert I came across Lily Marlene:

"Every time the line passed under the light of a street lamp, the eerily unreal autumn flowers shone on their arms and helmets. They waved over the threatening dark hue of the marching column like a benediction, mistakenly sent down by some invisible hand. . . ."

Wiechert's street lamp must be the same as that of the song. Under a lamp of this kind Lily Marlene saw the soldiers march by, and sought under the hundreds of identical helmets for the face of her young Franz. In the pages of *Jedermann,* like a gust of cold wind swirling through the broken ranks of a company of soldiers marching toward one last desperate battle and an autumnal defeat, there is the same anxiety as that which grips the heart of Lily's young man.

> *"Underneath the street lamp by the barrack gate,*
> *Darling, I remember the way you used to wait . . ."*

In both Wiechert's text and the grave notes of the song, I find the same melancholy, epical theme. Men are marching against fate; they know it, but they march on.

> *". . . Then, when the music stopped, nothing could be heard but the ceaseless, regular tread of the troops, with something fatal and threatening about it, in the nocturnal calm, and the hoofbeats of the horses on the cobblestones . . ."*

It recalls the end of "Lily Marlene," where the drums sound like tolling funeral bells: *Tam . . . Tam . . . Tam. . . .*

> *"Give me a rose, on my heart to wear;*
> *Tie it with a lock of your golden hair . . ."*

There are flowers in both places, autumnal flowers in *Jedermann,* spring flowers in "Lily Marlene." Thinking of the song, in these painful and uncertain days, I feel that its echo harmonizes with that of the book. History repeats itself, but at changing seasons.[1]

That is, if the reader admits that the sad notes of "Lily Marlene" contain a presage of some kind. When I heard it for the first time, the Germans were overrunning Europe and the whole world trembled before them. But I said to myself: "That's no war song; it voices some sad presentiment." As Wiechert says, "Something fatal and threatening. . . ."

Madness

December 10

Some men spend the day covering sheets of paper with plans and sketches. They rebuild the house, shift the furniture and debate the wisdom of carving a fireplace out of the living room. This is homesickness, pure and simple; it expresses a man's need to cast out a safety line linking him to the vital center of his life.

Some men throw themselves into lectures, and into historical, political, philosophical, artistic and literary discussions; they argue about Proust, Croce, Marx, Cézanne and Leopardi. This is the instinct of self-preservation; it reflects the necessity of injecting oxygen into the *Lager's* dank, stuffy air.

There are men that wander from hut to hut, from

---

[1] Actually, the war did end in May, two years later.

bunk to bunk, asking for opinions on the war, how long
it will last and what will come after. This may reveal a
certain weakness of character, but it is due in large part
to boredom and inanition.

Other men do nothing but think and talk about food.
And this is sheer madness. Of course we are hungry.
Hunger hovers over us at every hour of the day and
peoples our dreams at night. We accept it in a spirit of
resignation, as an inevitable and incurable ill.

But such men are on the way to going mad. Food is
the only subject of their conversation. They plan break-
fasts, lunches, dinners, snacks and midnight suppers.
They describe and invent sandwiches, draw up menus
for sensational banquets to be held after their return
home. They collect the names of good restaurants and
local delicacies and compile gastronomic guidebooks, or
else they write down and annotate recipes for the most
complicated dishes.

The futile chatter about things to eat and the futile
thought concentrated on eating only spur the appetite.
In these men's heated imaginations are bottomless pits,
with stomachs the dimensions of their desires.

This form of madness is fraught with anxiety. Its prac-
titioners acquire protruding bones; their faces are yellow from the fear of being hungry rather than from ac-
tual hunger.

Letter Home

They gave us our first form letter, a sheet with lengthy
German instructions and only a small space left for writing in Italian. The right-hand side of the sheet was to
serve for a reply and we were not to trespass upon it.
Furthermore, we were to use a pencil, to write clearly,
to stick to the dotted lines and, in short, to observe the
international conventions whose purpose is to safeguard
the rights of prisoners of every nationality.

We were also given a double, folding postcard, with
instructions in French. One half of this card, stuck to a
properly packed parcel, would ensure any such parcel's
exit from Italy and its transportation to our temporary
place of residence.

Captain N. told me, disquietedly, that we were allotted no more than twenty-four lines, and Captain C.
added that since these lines had to include directions for
sending a parcel, it was no laughing matter. "Brevity,
that's the keynote," put in Captain M. And so we set to
work, very concentratedly, pooling the results of our
individual efforts.

Captain N., who wanted news of his home and business, came up, after due reflection, with a first sample of
ingenuity: *Inform homelife office.* For this happy ab-
breviation he was judged equal to Captain C., who in-
structed his wife to send him his heavy uniform and all
possible winter clothing with a mere: *Send woolsuit
underwools.*

After these messages had been approved, we tackled

the more difficult problem of how to explain briefly the
rules for making up a well-wrapped parcel, weighing no
more than ten pounds, labeled with an enclosed sticker,
containing no playing cards, medicines or inflammable
liquids, but rather cigarettes, tobacco, barley and wheat
meal. This was a real challenge, but it was finally re-
solved by the following telegraphic formula: *Strongpack
tenpounder with insticker. No carddrugs inflammables
but cigtobacco, wheatmeal, barley.*

I was reminded of the want ads I had once scanned so
often, but the memory of them did not make me smile;
it only added to my homesickness. Tightly packed columns of newsprint, whose strange wording seemed to
have been dictated by a miserly telegraph operator, you
told us of respectable forty-year-olds wanting acquaint-
ances with view matrimony; shorthandtypists desirous
salary raise; hideaway apartments; singlerooms for office-
workers; heated, hotwatered furnished apartments for
govemployees. Yes, gray want ad columns, you vaunted
like new cars ready to roll over roads around blue lakes;
confidential detective agencies; big business deals; trustworthy pensioners; employment offers. . . . From behind this barbed-wire fence, my former amusement dies
away, and I only long to see you.

Gray, densely printed back pages, crazy literature at
ten liras a line, you had a poetry all your own, the
poetry of the workaday world, the rhythm of life!

As I listened to the hybrid words we had put together
for our form letters, I was filled with memories of the
want ad pages, and of a rhythm long since broken. I

imagined a big piece of miserably empty white paper, bearing at the bottom a single line, desperate message: *"Little boy searches every evening for his far-away father."*

*　　*　　*

"Strongpack tenpounder with insticker. . . ."

I was absorbed by thoughts of the want ad pages of the *Corriere della Sera,* of days long past, when I had scanned offers of shorthandtypists, singlerooms and hot-watered apartments. But I didn't laugh. I said to myself that the form letter was good enough for me and I would make use of it. Then I went away from the group and began to fill up with tiny print the twenty-four lines allotted to me. I wrote clearly, with a pencil, on the dotted lines, according to the international convention whose purpose is to safeguard the rights of prisoners of every nationality.

"My lady: *Strongpack tenpounder with insticker. No carddrugs, inflammables, but underwools, cigtobacco* . . . and dried chestnuts. But if you think the chestnuts would do more good to our little boy, please keep them for him. I don't really need anything. All I have to ask is this: that on Christmas Eve you set the table as gaily as you can. Get out the best silver and glasses, spread the embroidered tablecloth and light all the lamps. Set up a big Christmas tree, with as many candles as possible, and put a crèche near the window, just as you did last year.

"My lady, you must do all these things for me. Every night my thoughts leap over the barbed-wire fence. I know it is difficult for you to picture this exactly, for thoughts have no faces; they are no more than gusts of air. So picture me, myself, leaping over the barbed-wire fence. Picture a Giovannino as light as a dream and as transparent as the wind on a quiet, cold winter night.

"Every night, when the others are sleeping, I fly away, over the boundless silence of foreign lands and cities. Below me, everything is dark and sad, and I am in search of light and peace. I see the statue of the Madonna atop our Milan cathedral, but the streets and squares are no longer the same as they were before, and I have a hard time locating our fifth floor.

"My lady, don't call me reckless if I come in through the roof; you ought to approve of my prudence in shunning the battered stair. Besides, there's a hole in the roof, and I can arrive all the more quickly. I recognize the arrangement of our rooms and look for memories under the dust of the crumbled walls. But here, too, everything is dark and cold and sad. Only with the help of the moon can I hope to make out the pattern of the tapestries still hanging on the walls and the layout of the furniture, which I once knew so well.

"No one walks in the deserted streets, except Fear, disguised as the moon. On a shred of wallpaper from what used to be our front hall, I can make out a strange five-petal flower. My lady, do you remember when Albertino decorated the apartment with tiny hands dipped in indelible ink? I have searched in vain in my old office building for reminscences of days gone by; the building simply isn't there, and in its place is a grim pile of smoke-blackened rubble.

"Now, leaving the darkened city behind me, I am revisiting the spots where you and I were boy and girl together. Again, nothing but melancholy greets my eye. And so I come, at length, to the rude cottage where my remaining belongings and my earliest longings have come to rest. You are asleep, Albertino is alseep, my mother and father are asleep. Perhaps, in your sleep, all of you are searching for my unknown abode. Our city furniture is heaped up in disorder in the small, shadowy rooms, while up in the attic there are cases of my books, with the words frozen on the pages.

"My lady, in my pursuit of light and warmth and peace, I have found only cold and darkness; I cannot see my son's face, and even the lake shore is empty and un-lighted. Ruefully I fly back to the barbed-wire enclosure. Down on the hard bunk flop the congealed bones of No. 6865.

"My lady, on Christmas Eve, when my thoughts leap over the barbed-wire fence, they must find some bright, warm corner. I want to be dazzled with bright lights, I want to look upon your face and recover the peace I once knew. Otherwise, what fun is there in being a prisoner of war?"

At this point I broke off, with a distinct feeling that I had run through the twenty-four allotted lines. As a matter of fact, I had spread myself over the twenty-four lines of my side of the form letter, the twenty-four lines of the reply blank and the better part of five other forms that happened to be lying around. Conscientiously I scratched out the hundred and fifty odd lines that I had written and began all over:

"Strongpack tenpounder with insticker. No carddrugs, inflammables, but underwools, cigtobacco. . . ."

It occurred to me that the censor would suspect "tenpounder" of being some diabolical explosive device. And I came to the melancholy conclusion that when a fellow sits down to write home, he never knows what to say.

As I Would Write it Ten Years from Today

How many years ago? But there's no use counting the years that are dead and gone, no use counting any years, for that matter. Somebody Else is keeping track of both years past and years to come.

We put up a big Christmas tree and wrote the names of the presents on bits of paper. I got one marked TWO POUNDS OF NOUGAT, which made me very happy, because nougat has always been my passion.

After that Lieutenant Roberto Rebora read one of his own poems. I remember exactly how it went.

Toward Christmas, 1943
From the motionless watch kept by the houses
in the beloved street,
the bleak winter morning is born.

The moon lingers
over the torpid roof-tops,
moving across chimerical walls,
and the fabulous heart's memories of valleys,
of gardens heavy with compassion.
In the still dreaming streets,
there are hesitant human attempts
to apprehend reality. Mere whispered syllables.
The high heavens dully intercede;
there is a mute violence in the tangle
of lost images.
Space comes out of the awakened eyes,
fearful of
a word of praise. Cautiously
the earth will once more effect its beginning.
Now there is meaning in the names which wander
through streets
brushed by an abandoned Christmas.

At that time and place it was a magnificent poem; to-day I no longer understand it. Poetry is meant to be felt rather than understood.

Next I read some of my melancholy prose and Coppola played his own delicate compositions on the accordion.

Outside, the sky was clear and I thought of the coming day. In the shadows around the barbed-wire fence I fancied that all my future actions were lurking. Now I can see only my actions of the past, and I sigh nostalgically for *Lager* 333.

*　　　*　　　*

Last night, before I went to bed, a strange notion took

hold of me. Silently I opened the bedroom closet and took from its protecting cover the faded uniform I had worn ten years before. I put it on and buttoned the five gilt buttons. After a minute or two, I quite naturally could not hold my breath any longer, and the buttons burst loose like so many pellets from a shotgun. One of them bounced on a pillow and came to rest, like a shooting star, among the tangled hair of Albertino the second. Poetry and adiposity.

In Milan, after ten years: "The good old days at Beniaminovo!"

1944

The Watchtower

January 15, 1944

Wherever you look, there, in the background, is the tower, omnipresent and watchful like the eye of God. Of the God they say is on their side (*mit uns*) so very different from our God, with the harshly sounded name of *Gott* which they have fastened upon Him.

Eternal Danger

January 20

War stories, stories of Russia, Croatia, Albania, Montenegro, North Africa, of land and sea and sky. Here we live a thousand lives; the war is multiplied in a thousand different episodes. It is no longer a mere word, but a concept with numberless bits of terrifying, infernal evidence to support it, even for the benefit of those who have not experienced it directly.

But tomorrow these historical facts will be literary material. Critics will review war books rather than war. Just as in the case of Remarque's *All Quiet on the Western Front,* they will exclaim: "What a wonderful book!" And no one will think to say: "What a horrible war!"

Huts

January 29

The huts in which we live are like railway cars, buried above the wheels, in sand. One after the other, a whole train of them, that has foundered. It seems impossible that they should ever emerge and start moving. And yet that is exactly what, one day, they must do.

Hut No. 18

One of the myriad examples of wartime architecture: a dark wooden hut, with a ditch and a circular hillock around it. A long, low-ceilinged hut, under the infinite sky above the Polish plain.

Hut No. 18. A miniature Noah's Ark, drifting over a Flood of melancholy. With inside, every conceivable kind of creature, from a louse to a poet, from a rat to a former government employee.

Hut No. 18. When we entered it for the first time, we huddled near the door, struck dumb by the sight of the three rows of empty bunks, with our eyes wandering over the bare walls, the uneven, dusty floor and the windows that had neither shades nor shutters.

We stood there, with our duffle bags in our arms, like miserable immigrants, penetrating the bowels of the ship that is to carry them away. We remained speechless, and time stamped every passing second on the icy silence, as if it were pitilessly beating it into our heads. All of a sudden there was an outcry:

"Captain Novello's hammer!"

*   *   *

Here I must recall the world's most accursed tool, a nefarious mixture of monkey wrench, pincers, wire cutter, chisel, file, screwdriver, hatchet and pig's foot. Every cubic inch of this minotaur of the mineral kingdom had a different function from the next, and the whole thing was a hammer worthy of being reviled in some magazine devoted to the defense of the racial purity of its kind.

"Captain Novello's hammer!"

It was the hybrid product of the most detestable American pragmatism and the worst abstract aberrations of the school of Picasso. This damnable gadget had lived through exposure on the steppes. Its owner lost all the rest of his earthly goods but, thanks to the miraculous injustice which often regulates human affairs, the hammer was saved.

"Captain Novello's hammer!"

Such was the outcry that broke the icy silence and transformed Hut No. 18 into the eighteenth circle of Dante's Hell. There were eighty of us, and each one had need of hundreds of nails and tacks with which to arrange his personal and public belongings. At all hours of the day, and far into the night, the confounded sound of the hammer could be heard.

How many nails did it drive into the walls? Twenty thousand would be a conservative guess. Italians have an instinctive feeling for nails. Exile an Italian to the shade of the only palm tree in an endless expanse of desert, and the next day you will find his jacket hanging from a nail stuck into the trunk of this solitary piece of vegetation.

Yes, Italians can always put their hands on a nail. When my son was three months old and had never been out of his crib, I found him one day sucking a carpet tack. And in 1912, so the archives of Lomellina tell us, a baby was born with a nail in its hand.

"Captain Novello's hammer!"

How many times did Hut No. 18 echo to that damned cry? Every now and then there were new arrivals from other internment camps. As soon as they entered the hut, they put their baggage down on the floor and without a moment's hesitation asked for Captain Novello's hammer. They were always up-to-date and in possession of the very latest news. Thanks to some mysterious grapevine, every one of seventy different camps, none of which could possibly communicate with the other, called soup "hogwash," cigarettes "reefers" and the process of toasting bread "crisping."

No sooner, then, had our new friends arrived upon the scene than they began to ask around for the confounded hammer. And the hammer went on pounding, *bang, bang, bang,* like an infernal timepiece, scanning the minutes of our melancholy boredom by knocking us regularly over the head.

As you may have gathered, I hated the thing. The day when the hut was inspected and searched for forbidden tools, I could not resist playing a traitor's role and pushing it into plain sight in the middle of the table. The German soldier saw it, all right, but he only looked at it with a superior air. As a son of the land of pure Aryan tools, he would have been utterly disgusted by the slightest contact with any such bastard Anglo-Jewish contraption.

One day the thing split into two parts, because its pivot screw was gone. Needless to say, I was glad. Although it contained all the accessory tools necessary to make the repairs, it could not very well operate upon itself, any more than a pencil with a lead at one end and a penknife at the other can hope to make itself any sharper. Unfortunately, a six-foot ski trooper found a way to put it right.

"Captain Novello's hammer!"

I hid it among the straw of my pillow stuffing, but

that night I dreamed that a nail was piercing my neck, and waking up with a start I found the hammer had emerged from the pillow and was driving it in. The next night I tucked it away in the mattress, down by my feet. But this time my nightmare was more horrendous than ever. Torquemada himself, with a pair of red-hot pincers, was pulling off my big toe. Awakened by my own shriek of pain, I looked down and saw my toe in the pincers' grasp.

"Captain Novello's hammer!"

One day the hammer disappeared. Some people said that it had cast its vote for a new Republic of Italy, while others insinuated that it had died for love, swallowed up by a hole in the wall. Three weeks later it came back, quite obviously from a round of dissipations, only to be received like a prodigal son, petted, cleaned, polished and fed on fatted calf. At once, it began to hammer again, even more arrogantly than before, and we submitted to its tyranny.

We were shifted from one camp to another, and in our new abode, on the evening of May 5, 1944, a German sergeant caught it red-handed. Together with a lieutenant from Hut No. 67, it was threatening the life of a poor, innocent German nail. That was the end of the hammer. But every now and then, amid the tedium of a long afternoon or in the heart of the night, there is a strange knocking on the walls. The ghost of Captain Novello's hammer is calling for vengeance.

Signora Germania

Signora Germania, you have shut me into a barbed-wire enclosure and you mount guard to prevent me from getting out. But it's no use. I can't get out, that's true, but it's easy enough to get in. The barbed-wire is no barrier to my memories and my affections. And that isn't all. God, too, comes through the fence and teaches me things contrary to your regulations.

Signora Germania, you search my duffle bag and my straw mattress, all in vain. There's nothing you can lay your hands on, and yet I possess secret papers of capital importance: the blueprint of my house, a thousand images of the past and imaginings of the future.

And there is more. Hidden somewhere I have a map, on a scale of one inch to a hundred miles, where there is marked, quite exactly, the very spot where I shall rediscover my faith in divine justice.

You are bothered about me, Signora Germania, and all to no avail. The day when you lose your temper and use one of your powerful new weapons to stretch me flat on the ground, something will happen to surprise you. A new man will arise, a much more formidable man than I was before, and you won't have time to pin an identification tag upon him before he's up and away, over the barbed wire and gone from view.

That is the nature of man, Signora Germania. Outwardly he's easy enough to bully, but inside him there is another self, who bows only to God. And that, Signora Germania, is why you can't win.

Germans

February 3

They fill a pot with water, measure out the meat and the powdered extracts, close the airtight lid, light the gas and then, when a certain valve emits a whistling sound, the soup is ready.

Their way of making war is very much the same. Into the pot they cast human flesh, explosive powders, and extracts from manuals of military science, then they put on the lid of uncompromising discipline and wait for a whistle to tell them that it's all over.

Only the whistle doesn't blow, and the pot explodes into a thousand pieces.

February 12

Unforgettable voices, for instance, that of Lieutenant R., which is mannered from the start because of its typically soft, Venetian intonation, and dipped in molasses besides, so that everything he says seems to be written on sweet, sticky flypaper.

In the hut dozens of people are always talking at once, some in a pounding staccato, others in singsong, but most of them intermittently and with an intensity which varies from a loud racket to a low whisper, from an uproar to total silence. But Lieutenant R.'s talk is like water running out of a leaky faucet. Whenever the other voices are lowered, his can be heard above them.

It is like an embroidery design, now visible, now covered over by stitches, but always basically present.

Yes, I shall long remember the voice of Lieutenant R. He talks and talks, with precise emphasis and a sugar-sweet tone. And his talk is of beefsteaks and ravioli, of gamebirds on rice, of biscuits and sweetmeats and of the more prosaic things to be expected in a food parcel from home.

All the while I suffer, just as I used to suffer listening to the metallic voice which read out the propaganda menu of the day:

"First, the United States can't come into the war, because . . ."

"Second, the British fleet is paralyzed, because . . ."

The Crowd

Every individual is at his worst in a crowd. Perhaps this is why peoples willing to subordinate their own personalities to an iron discipline which whips them into a compact mass are more inclined than others to racial hatred and war.

Italians are not likely to follow any such trend. They are cut out to be its victims rather than its activators.

Rays of Light

February 20

Four black pearls gleam in his red heart. Four miniature black suns shine in the gray sky of his melancholy.
His children's eyes, which look out at him from every
corner.

Questions and Answers

There is a passionate interest in the problems of the
future. Some prisoners are always analyzing what is
wrong and coming to the conclusion that Italy's best
bet is to be like Switzerland.

Others (a great number) are madder still. They say
that Italy's only hope lies in world domination. They
can always point to the ancient Romans as an example.

Footsteps on the Sand

One night his daughter appeared to him in a dream and
said: "The war will be over, for you, in early March."
He told his fellow prisoners, and was extremely happy.

He had the same dream a month later, after he had

been for a week in the infirmary, where every night they found him out of his bed and wandering about like a ghost, in search of the music of *The God-maker,* an opera on which he had been working for years. Rejoicing again in his dream, he sent word of it to his fellows. "For me, the war will be over in early March."

Four days later, during the night of March 2, 1944, Captain Musella was dead.

He was a tiny, bent man. When he walked around the camp, it seemed as if the whole weight of the endless Polish sky were bearing down upon his sorrowfully stooped shoulders. Looking at him not merely as a prisoner but also as a musician, and thinking of his involvement with so weighty a theme as that of *The God-maker,* one couldn't help feeling that his shoulders, like those of Atlas, carried the whole world upon them. Actually, as a composer, he was equal to coping with things greater than himself, but as a prisoner he was crushed by the immensity of the leaden sky.

He had arrived at the beginning of January from the camp at Deblin, where on carefully glued-together envelope backs he had reconstructed Bach and Grieg scores, formed choruses and an orchestra and organized concerts for his fellow prisoners' pleasure. He was a tiny man, who looked sociable and talkative, but actually wanted more than anything to work, work, work, as if he were afraid he would not have time enough to write the music and words which were locked up in his brain. He talked and worked with us in the little theater of Beniaminovo, but he never did accomplish all he wanted because for him, in early March, the war was over.

* * *

In the late afternoon of March 3, 1944, a strong wind was blowing. On the frozen ground the prisoners stood in two long lines stretching from the infirmary to the door of the *Kantine*. A sorry assembly of strange clothes and strained faces.

First there was heard a mournful psalm, more like a fearsome threat, growing louder and louder in the silent air. Then, all of a sudden, against the muddy campsite, the unexpected, almost intrusive sight of the red, white and green flag, laid over the coffin. This was the second time we had had the privilege of seeing these colors, but the price we paid was too high. The first time was on February 9, when Captain Cipriano Colombini, was the first among us to leave the camp in this, the only way anyone could involuntarily leave it. That morning there was snow, but the bright colors seemed just as illogical and inadmissible against its whiteness as they did now against the dreary March afternoon. Whatever the time and the season, they represented to each one of us a reality so sharp as to conflict with our desperately evasive dreaming.

As the coffin moved along, swinging on the pallbearers' narrow shoulders, the prisoners found the unaccustomed energy to salute. There was a clicking of wooden shoes, as if the coffin were advancing through a narrow, frozen canal, opening a way through the ice before it.

The bark of death swung past, and ice crackled at my feet.

That night the wind froze, and hid in the woods to await the morning. The moon stood still and everything was motionless in earth and sky. Then it was that Death walked through the camp. No one could stop Death from entering; this was the only right conceded to men from whom all rights had been taken away. Death walked among the huts that night and told one wakeful man a singular story.

"In the *kantine* there is a coffin, and beside it the piano which is played at Mass. All of a sudden, a tiny man miraculously appears. He runs his transparent fingers over the keys and music comes out of them. He is practicing his composition; now, at last, he has found the score for which he searched in vain, as a ghost, in the infirmary."

That night Death walked through the camp, and those who were not sleeping heard footsteps on the sand and faraway music.

Six Months

March 9

Six months, six thousand days. Boredom so alters our apprehension of time that minutes are no longer fractions of an hour, but units of eternity.

Kneeling on the sand to wash the soup buckets, I take a look at my hands, which are unrecognizably different from what they were before, blue from cold, with a network of taut muscles and gnarled, swollen veins. There is a permanent layer of grease on the skin and the tips of the thumb and forefinger are black from cigarette butts smoked down to the point of burning.

As I go to pump water from the well, it seems as if the two buckets would pull my arms out of their sockets and under their weight I should sink up to my knees in the sand. As I wash my hands, I discover a bony structure which seems to belong to a total stranger. Staring into a puddle of water, I see floating above my head clouds so distant and indifferent that they might belong to a different world, to a world where other men have resumed their normal life, while we forgotten ones continue our futile and accursed round.

When I sit down at the table to write, my back aches, and the words weigh me down like buckets of sand.

Six months, six thousand days. My calendar is filled with dead days, each one marked by a penciled cross. I think back to the unhappy years I spent in boarding-school, to the dreary months at the military academy. Then, too, I marked every passing day with a cross, but I knew that there was an end in sight, exactly five years and six months away. Here I know nothing. It's like emptying bags of cement into a bottomless hole in the ground. How many bags to fill the hole, one or ten thousand?

When it's all over, some men will have proud medals

to pin on their chests. But on our worn tunics we shall
pin only the penciled crosses that mark our dead days.

Short Short Story

March 12

Beyond the barbed-wire fence, a little man from Turkestan, in a green jacket, is running. From where I
kneel on the sand, washing the soup buckets, I can see
outside the enclosure three huts (two to the right and
one to the left), a second fence, and in the distance a
long line of low, dark green trees. Above, a gray sky,
like that of 1914–18.

A little man from Turkestan, in a green jacket, is
running. He calls out something like "hello" and, without stopping, throws me half a loaf of bread. He runs on,
a slight, smiling figure, teaching, by example, a lesson
from one of my old school copybooks.

Return

March 15

A hand has taken hold of my stomach and is trying
to wrench it out of my body. For a moment it loosens
its grip, only to tighten it again, a moment later.

This same hand caused me the same pain twelve months ago. I can still feel my mouth sticky with milky barium and see, on a photographic plate, the little blob in the center of a circle. In those days my bureau was crowded with boxes and bottles of medicine and measuring cups and glasses. Even food can be a medicine of sorts, in which case it is prescribed in definite doses.

Here, two soldiers arrive at noon with a great steaming bucket; they slide it off the pole on which they carried it and deposit on the floor. There are men that shout with joy over the arrival of the soup and eagerly watch over the filling of the aluminum bowls lined up on the table. As for me, I might as well swallow cement, and there is nothing I can do but take refuge on my bunk.

Once more I am crying. My thirty-five years stare at me in amazement, and I feel as if I were looking on at the tears of a child.

I see a man walking down a familiar, dusty country road, with a knapsack over his shoulder. The ditch running alongside the road is filled with bracken water. The echo of a church bell still floats in the still air and a rooster is crowing. There, as here, it is high noon.

The man stops in front of a closed gate. Who will be the first to appear in the dark rectangle of the doorway? He stands motionless. The shadow of the closed gate falls upon the white, dusty road, but the figure of the man casts no shadow.

Crying again. I feel as if I were abandoned by everyone, including myself, since my body seems to me to

belong to times long since gone by. I wait in vain for
someone to appear at the door. Between myself and the
people of this house, between my ghost and life, there
is a veil of tears, and everything seems written on trem-
ulous water.

A Prisoner's Spring

The few potatoes that they literally hand out to us every
day have long, wormlike white tendrils. It must be
Spring.

The Dream

Our only privilege is to dream. Dreaming is necessary
to us, because our life is outside the barbed-wire enclosure, and we have no way of getting there except in
our dreams. Only through them can we maintain a hold
on reality and remember that we are still alive. After
futile days, measured by ounces of food and numbers of
cigarette butts, dreams offer us the only real activity
we know. Dream we must, for in our dreams we recover
forgotten values and find new ones we had never known
before; we detect the errors of our past and catch a
glimpse of the future.

Let us sit outside the hut and project the visions of our desire upon the open sky. Let us dream, with clear heads and open eyes; let us write our own plot and scenario and be directors, actors, cameramen and spectators of our own imaginary story.

I don't know how I came to this place and there is no use my trying to find out, since dreams are not furnished with information bureaus. All I know is that the square where a man in semi-military uniform with a knapsack over his shoulder is walking, is the one in front of the station of my native city, Parma.

But I do know one very important thing, I am that man. I caught a glimpse of myself as I leaned over to catch my reflection in the fountain at whose center the statue of Vittorio Bottego, the explorer, flanked by two bronze savages, is wondering whether it was really worthwhile to penetrate the upper waters of the Omo and the Juba.

Against the light I see the whole city in profile. Directly ahead, seeming to enfold me in a huge cement embrace, is the great birthday-cake monument to Giuseppe Verdi.[1] The composer takes no notice of me. From the bas-relief of the central altar he continues to look nervously toward the station, as if he were awaiting the arrival of the suitcase in which he packed his suit and hat. Obviously, he is tired of playing the part of an allegorical figure, stark naked and with an uncomfortable broad-brimmed laurel wreath on his head.

---

[1] This monument was demolished after the Anglo-American occupation, partly because it was damaged, but largely to celebrate the new freedom.

The Operas—of both sexes—ignore me also, standing on pedestals at the foot of every column of Ximenes' architectural effort and restraining with their cemented immobility the bronze irritation of the Master. Only the chorus from *Nabucco,* a solitary gentleman standing apart from the others in the semicircle, whispers something in my ear. (The sun makes the dew on the rooftops glitter, and there is gold dust in the air.) Yes, old Nebuchadnezzar, you were right to speak of

". . . *the gentle air of one's native land. . . .*"

*   *   *

I enter the still sleeping city and my footsteps on the deserted cobblestones awaken a sign which had been asleep, leaning against a column.

PEDESTRIANS SHOULD KEEP TO THE SIDEWALKS, it grumbles ill-humoredly.

I beseech it to calm down, to let me enjoy the sun. For such a very long time I have dreamed of walking down the middle of a sunlit street. After all, I'm just back from an internment camp.

"Yes, but you've come back on foot and so, as far as I'm concerned, you're a pedestrian and have to obey the regulations!"

*   *   *

I am walking between the trolley rails, across the silent, deserted square. As I proceed toward the beginning of the narrow street which leads to the outskirts of the city, someone calls out:

"Giovannino, aren't you even going to say hello to

your old café? Pick a wicker chair out of the heap and sit down. Half an hour from now the waiter will be here to open up. Then, later on, you'll see the proprietor, the barmaid, the blond cashier and your friends. Let's have a bit of a talk while you're waiting. If you could have heard half the things your friends have said about you . . ."

"That's quite enough, old café. All I care about is what they've been thinking at home. I was imprisoned for the sake of my family, not that of my friends, and it's for their sake that I've returned."

*   *   *

I go on down the quiet, shaded street, and my footsteps on the deserted cobblestones awaken an echo that was fast asleep beneath an ancient arcade.

"Tap . . . tap . . . tap. . . . Hello there, Giovannino! I know your step. You've walked for so long on yielding sand that you've forgotten that your footsteps have a distinctive pattern. Now it's exactly the same as it was before, when you used to emerge at dawn from the printer's and go home, walking, just as you are now, over the deserted cobblestones. All this time I've kept the sound of your footsteps in a crack in the wall. Tap . . . tap . . . tap. . . . Do you hear?"

At the edge of the city I come out onto the broad, sunny boulevard.

"Stop, Giovannino," whispers a horse-chestnut tree. "You used to lean against me when you were waiting for her, don't you remember?"

"Giovannino, I'm your bench," murmurs an old stone

seat. "Sit down and tell me about yourself, and about her. And I'll tell about both of you. . . ."

There are still three miles to go, across country, before I get home. And so, without stopping, I answer:

"Goodbye, Youth, goodbye. . . ."

Here is the dusty, white road, with the telegraph poles all in a row. There is a festive whispering in the air.

"Welcome home, Signor Giovannino!" say the hedge, the trees, the grassy ditch.

All these are good, old-fashioned, country things, which address me respectfully. They speak to me as I pass and try to persuade me to linger. They want to give me something, but they are afraid. They knew me when I was a child; they made me presents of violets, blackberries, and round, flat stones. One day an elm tree gave me a baby bird and a ditch gave me a dragonfly that seemed to be made of glass. But now I am grown up and wear a mustache; they no longer dare offer me a plum or an acacia leaf to make into a whistle under my tongue. Just to show my appreciation, I take a blade of grass to chew.

Chewing the blade of grass, I walk on. Around the next curve I shall suddenly see my own house; when it hears my voice it will wake up abruptly and gaze with astonishment out of all its windows. Just at the curve, there is a wayside shrine, with a bench in front of it, and someone calls from very far away: "Giovannino!"

"Old Grandmother Giuseppina, why have you left your peaceful, grass-covered tomb and come so far? I would have come to you, Grandmother Giuseppina, bearing the flower I gathered in that desolate, distant land. I have it right here, pressed in my wallet, Grandmother Giuseppina; I would have brought it to you and told you the whole story."

"I know, Giovannino, but I didn't have the patience to wait, and so I came to meet you."

"Have you been waiting so long, Grandmother Giuseppina?"

"Ever since you went away. For months I've been talking about you with this kind Madonna. She knows you just as well as I, from the time when you passed by here day after day, as a schoolboy, with your bag of books over your shoulder. Give her your flower. My grave has flowers of every description growing on it. There's even a red poppy, which I'll give you if you come to see."

"I'll come, Grandmother Giuseppina."

I lay my dried flower in the box standing on the shelf in front of the Madonna, and the corolla re-opens and takes on as bright a color as if it had been picked just a minute ago.

"Goodbye, Giovannino. Don't gulp too much cold water. And better put your cap back on."

Hobbling along with the aid of her cane, Grandmother goes back across the fields, by the same way she came. Now my house is in sight.

"Don't run, Giovannino," calls back Grandmother Giuseppina. "You're too weak to exert yourself."

In a minute I shall shout something or other, I still

don't know what. And my voice will sound like the
chorus of La Scala.

*   *   *

And so Giovannino has finally come home. But at
this very moment he finds himself in a dilemma. The
last scene is of capital importance. It would be a complete waste of time to have suffered for months and
months, with only sentimental illusions to sustain him,
and then to ring down the curtain on a fiasco. The matter requires thought.

His first idea of making a loud noise is quickly dis-
carded. By so doing he would inflict a rude shock upon
good people who need to be quietly awakened from the
bad dream which has for so long held them in thrall.
Making gentleness his aim, Giovannino edges his way to
a point just below the bedroom window, and in a faraway, positively dreamlike voice, calls the name of his
better half. A moment later a blind goes up, and a
sleepy face looks out. There she is!

After a moment of total and utter surprise, her half-
shut eyes open as wide as headlights. Her head is with-
drawn, and there comes a loud shriek:

"He's here!"

What happens next is something like the French
Revolution. The first shriek is answered by a second,
and the second by a third, each one farther away than
the last. Then comes a shriek from nearby and one from
still nearer, inaugurating the Reign of Terror.

Padlocks creak, chains rattle, doors slam: there are

dull thuds, meows, barks, ringing bells, crackling words and ear-piercing shouts. Albertino bursts out of bed and, catching his foot in his nightshirt, rolls down two flights of stairs. His dear mother tries to catch him, but slips on a ball, inadvertently grabs the leg of the table holding the goldfish bowl and falls to the floor in a splash of water, while the slimy little fish tumble down the neck of her dressing gown, their tails flailing madly.

The cat is quick to take advantage of this state of affairs and throws herself upon the slimy prey. Giovannino is faced not by his wife, but by a seething mass of hair, fish and catcalls. Meanwhile his old father, unable to adjust his eyeglasses, is groping his way toward the door. Finding a knob before him, he turns it and stumbles into the china cupboard. The crash of china awakens Giovannino's mother and, because she imagines there must be an earthquake, she calls out that everyone's first thought must be not for her but for the children.

The baby girl, whom all have forgotten, climbs out of her crib and onto the floor. She finds the bell which opens the front door and pushes the button so often that it seems as if all the express trains of Central Europe were arriving together.

"No, no," sobs Giovannino, before the smoking ruins of his family. "This will never do!"

Everything is wrong, everything must be done over. He must backtrack, like a moving-picture reel, rewound from the end to the beginning.

The baby girl regains altitude and goes back to bed.

The old father emerges from the china cupboard, the fragments of china resume the shape of plates, cups and saucers, and leap up to the shelves. The table leg straightens, the goldfish fly into the bowl, the wife reconquers the dignity of an upright position, Albertino rolls upstairs and the window closes. Giovannino's words reenter his mouth, letter by letter, and he falls upon the grass, holding his head between his hands.

"Lord help us! How hard it is to come home!"

The Clipping

April 16

I pace up and down, from one side of the fence to another; I move quickly, but hunger stalks me. Every mark on the sand is the trace left by a man's footstep or a man's thought. My footsteps and thoughts are superimposed upon a thousand others.

I fly over the nearby fence and over faraway mountains, until my desperate desire comes down in familiar ground. The central square of my native city is golden with sunshine, and umbrellas are raised over the café tables. There sit my friends, watching the pretty girls go by. Warmth fills the air. The happy memory of bygone days looks out at me from the faces and walls that meet my eye. But hunger impinges upon my thoughts and drives me away from the square and down a side street nearby.

"Bread, bread!" it cries. "You want white bread, fragrant from the oven, so fresh that it crumbles between your fingers."

I come across one bakery after another, even in localities where I have never seen them before.

Bread! Bread! The slicer screwed onto the heavy beechwood table moves up and down, cutting loaf after loaf, which delivery boys carry away in baskets balanced on their shoulders.

As I pace from one side of the fence to another, my feet trample crisp loaves of bread instead of yielding sand. Stalking hunger kneads my stomach and steam from the oven beclouds my eyes. I quicken my step, attempting to lose myself in the byways of memory. I want to cry out that I am hungry, but I am afraid to hear my own voice, and I start running. But hunger is right at my heels.

Bread, milk and cheese. Hunger restores a taste for simple foods, just as distance creates a desire for all that is pure and eternal. Hunger and sorrow cleanse both soul and palate; they drive a man back to life's original sources.

Bread, milk and cheese, and all the while my mouth is full of rancid spittle, and my jaw muscles ache. How many more hours before they can chew? Five hours, and then we shall have a couple of potatoes and a bowl of turnip soup. At once, my stomach will be aware of the trick that has been played upon it and ache even more violently than before. Already I can imagine the hunger that follows the meal.

As I pace from one fence to another, I clench my jaws, but the cursed wind whistles through my empty stomach as through a shell abandoned on the shore. The cursed northern air penetrates my every pore; I am an empty bag, and the wind whirls around inside. No matter how fast I go, hunger follows. In desperation I push my heart over the barbed-wire fence, where the early-morning sun reminds me of mornings gone by.

The sun streams into my faraway house. Albertino wakes up, and his eyes—two tiny black suns—peer over the edge of the pale blue crib alongside our bed. (Now, beyond the barbed-wire fence, amid a field of green barley, a lark rises, singing, vertically into the air, then stops flapping his wings and glides against the wind, without a pause in his song. He is like a jet of sparkling water, fanning out at the summit of its upward spurt like a crystal flower. The trills of the motionless bird are like clear water drops, that fall, like flower petals, laden with sun and song, to the ground below.)

The trill comes from the pink crib, on the other side of the bed, where Carlotta has opened her eyes to greet her hundred and sixtieth day.

Women pass among the farmhouses, carrying baskets of fragrant white bread; men pour buckets of creamy, foaming milk into the heavy zinc cans in which they will travel to market. Nearby, one fellow is beating butter, still not fully clotted as it comes out of the churn.

A boy walks toward the fields, eating a slice of buttered bread and a handful of nuts.

Hungry! Yes, hungry, that's what I am! To the matutinal longings of my heart are added the matutinal rumblings of my stomach. I pace up and down, but hunger still breathes down my neck. I swallow a mixture of air and saliva, while my hands vainly search my pockets. Not a grain of tobacco, not for days. A good smoke might drive hunger away, but cigarettes are only to be obtained by bartering bread. It's an infernal vicious circle.

The sentry gazes indifferently out of the watchtower, the lark sings on in the sky, and the sky is filled with wind and sun. It's quite useless for me to tell my sorrow to the soldier, the bird, the sun, the wind, the sky, for they are German, all of them. Everything around me is alien and inimical.

Back in the hut, I throw myself down on the blankets piled up on my bunk and whisper my shame to my neighbor.

"I'm hungry," I gasp.

Without a word, he hands me a clipping from an Italian newspaper, which served to stuff a recently received food parcel.

"When will interned Italian officers weary of eating buttered rolls at the expense of our German allies?"

Instinct

In front of Hut No. 29, a prisoner is vainly trying to split a piece of wood with a chisel. A German captain arrives upon the scene and starts an animated conversation, expressed chiefly in sweeping gestures. The prisoner fails to understand and throws out his arms in despair, then shrugs his shoulders and goes back to the job. The German walks away, but returns a moment later with an Italian lieutenant in tow. A short distance away the lieutenant had been struggling to split another piece of wood with a hammer.

Now it's all perfectly clear. If the two join forces, both of them can achieve their aims. What impelled the German to bring them together? Kindness? No, just the German instinct for organization, the fatal instinct that periodically inspires the Teutons to try to organize the whole world.

Shipwreck

April 20

Snatches of song, remembered names of men and institutions, inconclusive greetings from one prisoner to another, these things float upon the sea of sand and tar by which we languish like the spars of some enormous shipwreck.

Prisoners, Soviet Style

April 22

All day long the "Volga-Volgas," as we call them, have been going by. High-wheeled wagons, loaded with barrels of dung, are carried out of the camp and dumped into huge holes dug either amid the green barley or the black peat. The wagons are pulled by teams of five, six or seven couples of Italian or Russian soldiers, hitched to them like oxen to the plow.

The Russians have a way of dramatizing the whole affair. They trudge slowly and with a gloomy air, as if the barrels contained the miseries of the entire universe.

The Russian uniform is suited more to a prisoner than to a soldier: long, drab, khaki overcoats and fur caps. The men's faces are strange and impenetrable, the eyes expressionless and the lips mute. They carry a mess bowl, attached to a piece of string hung around their shoulders. Over them there hangs an air of deportation, of Siberia. It seems impossible that such men should ever fight battles or win a war.

The Pond

April 23

In one section of the camp, there are only a few scattered huts, and a puddle of water which might almost be

called a pond. Around it there are banks some six feet
high, and grass growing on the far side of the still, black,
oily, tar-like water. Four or five huts and two power-
line poles are mirrored in its depths; this is the only
example of coquetry to be found anywhere in the Lager.
The sky is never mirrored, for it hardly has an existence
of its own. Its neutral gray color seems intended only to
frame the romantic gloom (nineteenth-century etching
style) of this landscape, which to some extent justifies
the inhabitants' periodical attempt to embark on the
conquest of kindlier climes.

Men scramble, like chickens, around the edge of the
pond. They are looking among the refuse for bits of coal
with which to build a fire to cook great pots of rice and
beans, almost certain to be vomited during the following night.

The scene is reminiscent of the outskirts of a big
western European industrial city, with its helter-skelter
agglomeration of miserable, dirty, gasoline-can huts and
an atmosphere redolent of naphtha, tar, filth and general melancholy.

Officers of every age search among the refuse, with
their figures reflected in the muddy water, while the
passing German soldiers mutter unintelligibly to themselves as they pass quickly by.

Cesspool

April 25

Everything about the Lager is logically planned, and so the opening of the cesspool is not *immediately* adjacent to the latrines.

They left the opening uncovered for two or three days because they wanted to pump up something with which to fill the dung barrels and fertilize the fields.

Many men, a dozen perhaps, slipped and fell halfway in. Today a ski trooper, submerged almost to the arm-pits, seemed to be suffering punishment in some circle of Dante's Hell.

Gymnastics

April 28

In front of his hut, a captain executes bends, push-ups and other gymnastic exercises. The seriousness of his every movement, the dignity of his tall, well-built body and the staring look in his Byzantine-mosaic eyes endow his efforts with the solemnity of some exotic rite.

Every morning, in front of the hut, the captain goes through this performance, with a little crowd collected around him. The onlookers shake their heads and throw out their arms in incredulity.

"The fellow must be crazy!"

"He doesn't *have* to do it, does he?"

"Why in heaven's name? . . ."

For some reason, the sight seems to irritate and even enrage them. Finally one fellow calls out:

"Afraid of getting fat, are you?"

The Portrait

April 30

Coppola has made a painstaking pencil sketch of me. At last I see myself as others see me. Decidedly, I am not the old Giovannino.

On my pre-war identification papers there is an un-shadowed, round face, so skillfully touched up by the photographer that not even the trace of a wrinkle is showing. The face has a blank expression and two stupidly staring eyes, like those of an advertising model, and the hair is well combed and wavy. You would think that I had just come back from some spa or health resort.

How different things are now! The layer of fat is gone, the skin is dry, and the lower jaw, freed of the excess baggage of a double chin, reveals a decisive and not unpleasing line. The cheekbones stand out sharply and exercise the structural function for which they were intended. Now there are shadows on my face; my eyes are larger and more mobile and alive. My hair is no longer enslaved to convention, but ruffles up from a noticeably higher forehead. A heavy, black mustache puts the final touch on my new face, neutralizing the excessive width of the nostrils. My neck has lost its thickness and my head is clearly detached, the way it should be, from my body. No longer do I look like a village idiot or a German, with my head seeming to grow right out of my shoulders. Indeed, my whole body has recovered the supple lines of its youth. Only the bagginess of the seat of my pants recalls the horrors of my fatty past.

I used to thoroughly dislike my looks and make fun of my clumsiness, even in humorous magazines. Now I am quite reconciled and, when I see myself in the mirror, I say with a cordial smile:

"Hello there, old man! If good friends don't die, they're bound to meet again!"

The Amateur Chef

The amateur chef is not so much a man as he is a collection of receptacles. He is a general assembly of boxes, a congress of jars, a world fair of pots and pans. In short, the amateur chef is not an individual, he is an industrial complex.

Every edible object that he receives is the object of earnest study, leading up to a detailed plan of action. Alternating procedures of fracturation and agglomeration, he manages to handle every day some forty containers of various kinds, with ingredients from all over creation.

As soon as he has got hold of his daily ration, he lays his materials on a board and starts composing. Out of blood sausage, cocoa, margarine, breadcrumbs and mashed potatoes, seasoned with a pinch of salt, a few drops of oil, a sprinkling of syrup and a bit of chestnut flour, there comes an impressive meat loaf.

Mixing turnip slices with sugar, canned milk, lard, a bouillon cube, two spoonfuls of Mellin's Baby Food, two of marmalade, some browned potato skins and flour, he produces croquettes which he then proceeds to fry in margarine and a blend of nameless canned fish and herb tea.

The amateur chef is not a man, he is a laboratory for chemico-gastronomical experimentation. He spends all his days beating, kneading, grating, stirring, browning, baking, roasting, simmering, shaping, frying, breading, straining, rolling, grinding, pouring, grilling, spreading, powdering, cutting and . . . waiting.

At eight o'clock in the evening he finally sits down at the table. At nine o'clock he is dead tired and goes to bed. Finally, at ten, he is awakened by the necessity of throwing up everything he has eaten.

The Miracle

May 1

Out of the crowd swarming in the vicinity of the barbed-wire fence in expectation of roll call, there emerges the yellowish wind jacket of Rebora. From the worn collar of Rebora's jacket emerges Rebora's head, which looks unusually large because it is balanced atop such a thin neck. And from one jacket sleeve, I can see the tips of Rebora's fingers, closed around a little pink package. In these days, Rebora resents the universe's indifference toward him, and there is an aggressive tone in his voice.

"I have an idea it's your birthday," he mutters, passing the pink package to Giovannino. "Here."

The package contains cigarettes, rationed cigarettes.

On this wind-beaten, sandy shore, buffeted by the dark waves of boredom, there is the flotsam and jetsam cast up by the terrible storm that has broken the lives of so many men. And all of a sudden, quite miraculously, out of this shapeless, dirty mass of humanity, there emerges something clean and pure, something that is a sign of civilization. Someone has remembered a friend and the ways of friendship. And he has infused a note of poetry into an overpowering quantity of sordid prose.

But then, after all, Rebora is a poet.

Why War?

May 7

Three prisoners—a Russian, a Frenchman and an Italian—are going through the hut to repair the boarding of the bunks. Directing them is a German corporal. None of the four knows a word of any language beside his own, and yet they hold long discussions and understand one another.

Among common soldiers, simple, unschooled fellows, it is always this way. It is culture that breeds misunderstanding.

Birthday

May 14

Today is my son's fourth birthday. In him I relived my childhood, and now this is taken away. I count his days rather than my own, and even if I am a prisoner I wish that time could have a stop.

Spring without Sun

May 20

This morning there was a surprise. The big green field

to the east of the barbed-wire enclosure was suddenly tinted with brown. The barley has begun to sprout.

Is it possible that under this cold, evil, sunless sky the seed has accomplished the miracle of multiplication? Does it, like everything else in this place, obey the laws of man rather than those of nature?

The melancholy teams of "Volga-Volgas" move now among a mass of waving grain, as if upon a stormy sea. Only the heads of the men yoked to the shafts and the tops of the wagons are visible, like spars of a shipwreck, from the shore.

Despair

May 25

In the bright stillness of noon, under a colorless sky, among the inflexible, geometrical outlines of the camp buildings and the desolation of the sand, despair is no longer of the earth but hangs, suspended in the air, penetrating the emptiness of our abandoned existence. Every man in the camp breathes it in; what started as an individual ill is soon a general obsession. It is not sorrow or anxiety, but despair.

Captain X has just had news that his only daughter, fourteen years old, died in Florence forty days ago. Despair. His friends took him by the arms and shoulders to prevent him from dashing at the fence and tempting the sentry to shoot him down. They are still holding him, but it is no longer necessary, for now his gesture of rebellion is to stand, with taut nerves, immovable as a stone. He does not tremble but seems to vibrate all over, as if he were made out of glass, like the wide-open eyes out of which he stares into space. Surely, at any moment, he may crack or shatter.

Despair, that is to say, the oppressive, unbearable feeling of total impotence.

Men have become so used to the monotony of their days that they imagine life outside has come to the same halt. That fate has suspended its laws, and nothing will happen before they go home. Then, all of a sudden, this illusion is violently broken.

In the outside world, life and death go on as usual. The prisoners feel as if they were left by the roadside while others continue their way, moving so far ahead that there is no way to overtake them.

We, the Living

May 28

Abruptly, with the awkwardness characteristic of everything that transpires in this land, a sunny day follows upon a hundred days of wind and rain. The sun is so warm that it melts the tar on the roof of the huts and makes it burning hot inside.

Men throw off the ragged clothes that like bark have enclosed them and lie down on the sand to dry the winter dampness out of their bodies.

Bones in the sun. Hollow bellies, protruding ribs, knotty joints, collarbones that look as if they were coming through the skin. All these are reminiscent of pictures in old medical books or the captions under photographs in the French magazine, *L'Illustration:* "Victims of the plague in Kuantung. . . . Aspects of the famine in India. . . ."

Disappointment

May 29

Sun and wind, between them, have dried up the "pond." The black water and the play of reflections upon it gave the illusion of some mysterious, subterranean life, seen through a window which opened upon a world different from our own.

Here is another disappointment. No longer can we find escape by plunging our thoughts into these supposed depths, which now are laid bare as nothing but an ordinary sandy bottom. Men stand on the bank as if they were before a door which they knew would never open again.

Close Shaves

May 30

All winter they grew mustaches, sideburns and beards of every length imaginable. Now they are all busy with Gillette razors. It's not really a desire for cleanliness, but simply the old Italian mania for self-punishment.

The "Chicken"

Last night I saw an old acquaintance. I refer to Albertino, who invaded my life exactly three years, five months and thirteen days ago, after I had given up my bachelor's independence in favor of matrimony. Now I had not seen him for some time. But before telling you how our encounter came about, I must explain something of the nature of dreams.

I, Giovannino, formerly a fat man and still a sentimental one, dream exactly the same way you do. I assume a horizontal position, close my eyes and fall asleep. While I sleep, I have visions of persons, things and places of a kind all their own. I have strange adventures, and from the filing cabinet of my brain I dig out a whole world of emotional and intellectual experiences.

Every one of these adventures is like a documentary film, with a soundtrack that we usually keep stored in

our memory. In dreams our subconscious is the operator. He may juggle a hundred different reels, cut them
up, mix the fragments and then glue them together into
a work of art which he then projects upon the screen of
our sleep. Before morning he puts everything back in
order, for the benefit of the day operator, a much more
ordinary and conventional fellow, whose name, in my
case, is Giovannino.

Grown men dream this way because the world in
which they have lived is stored away in their brain. But
not so children, for their filing cabinets are still empty,
or else contain only a few very simple things: likenesses
of their mother, father and grandparents, of a pet kitten,
a yellow flower, a gold button, a white horse. Because
Albertino's subconscious has no world of its own and
can find no documentary film to project, it breaks out
and enters the world of others.

Just look at a child, sleeping quietly in his narrow
crib, under the velvety light of a night lamp. While he
lies there, so very still, something white and transparent
comes out of his body; it is another child, in his image,
made of light and air, or rather, it is his subconscious
embarking upon a separate existence, in the night world
of other people.

So the sleeping child dreams until, at dawn, his ghostly
image returns and is one with him again. In the filing
cabinet, where there was nothing but a white horse
before, Albertino finds a film that depicts a white horse
flying through the sky. When he opens his eyes, he tells

his familiars that he has ridden on a white horse to the moon.

This is how it came about that last night I saw Albertino. I was dozing in the upper chamber of my "castle," with my fellow prisoners sleeping soundly around me, when suddenly, in the ray of light streaming through a crack in the paper over the window, I saw a tiny figure, apparently made of moonstuff. He was standing, clad in a long nightshirt, where my potbelly used to be; he had curly hair and a piratical expression. Albertino had come, in his dreams, to look for his father, for the man that had made him a son.

He stared at me in perplexity, and I asked him where he was going. He said that he was searching for his father, and I said that I was he, at the same time moving my face into the ray of light. He gazed at me gravely and ran his fingers over my hollow cheeks. I inquired discreetly about the other members of the family, and he gave me all sorts of interesting news. His grandfather made a face like a lion, his grandmother told the story about the three little pigs and his mother threatened him all the time with the most dreadful punishments.

"What does she say?" I asked him.

"She says that if I'm a bad boy, the Germans will come and eat me up."

"Quietly there, Albertino! The enemy is listening."

I pulled him underneath the blanket. The ray of light fell on one corner, where there was stamped an imperial German eagle, with its wings spread out, ready to fly.

"Chicken?" he asked me.

"Here's hoping, Albertino!"

For a long time we whispered to each other. He told me about a bunch of flowers that bloomed afresh every day in a glass set before an ancient and unspeakably benign face of the Redeemer. Then he searched the pocket of his nightshirt and pulled out a green rubber ball, a gold button and a key from my old typewriter.

"I have a gun, too," he told me.

"I only wish I could say the same!"

I pushed up the paper which served as a blind over the window and saw the first signs of dawn in the sky.

"Go home, Albertino," I said. "Mother's waiting."

"What about you?" he asked.

"I'll be coming along," I said. "Tomorrow. *Morgen.*"

He emerged from under the blanket, shaking his head, and waved bye-bye with his transparent hand. I raised the blind and saw that it was nearly light outside. Albertino fluttered in the air overhead, then set his course due southwest. He hovered a moment above the Sanctuary.

"What are you up to, silly?" I wondered.

Cautiously I opened the window. Then I saw ten, a hundred, a thousand other Albertinos fly out of the camp windows and gather together over the belltower before, like an army of doves, they winged their way toward the sunlit south. Suddenly a big trimotor plane descended upon them out of the upper regions of the sky. I choked down an anguished cry. But the army of doves remained unbroken.

No one can intercept a prisoner's dreams. The doves

flew on, the sky took on a pale blue color and I re-
joiced in my heart. There was going to be another
beautiful autumn day.

Royal University of Sandbostel

June 3

The German June begins with a cold, rainy, autumnal
day. The sky seems to be aware of the gravity of the
times in which we are living; it is as surly as the race of
northern men, whom from birth to death it oppresses.

The university courses, which were to have begun
yesterday, have been postponed until the return of good
weather. The university has a well-ordered schedule and
a topnotch faculty, but no roof over its head. A little
group of men seated on the ground behind Hut No. 3
is the Law School; behind No. 7 the Humanities; behind No. 10, Engineering, then Agriculture, Account-
ing, and the rest.

In the watchtower across from the Humanities, a sentry listens indifferently to a passage from Dante, every
word of which is unintelligible to him.

> *"Some there I marked, as high as to their brow*
> *Immersed, of whom the mighty Centaur thus:*
> *'These are the souls of tyrants, who were given*
> *To blood and rapine. Here they wail aloud*
> *Their merciless wrongs. . . .'"*

White Collar

June 10

Another miracle, something pure and unspotted, such as one might expect to see if a hand had emerged from the lowering clouds and sprinkled whitewash over the drab mass of six thousand ragged men.

Today, Navy Day, there was a solemn Mass in the chapel, with a white-gloved Marine at either side of the altar and the senior officer of the camp in the front pew, standing as squarely on his feet as if he were at the helm of his ship. The few men who brought any baggage with them wore a white shirt and their best uniform. The others, who came in sweaters and sandals, searched the collection of miscellaneous gear they had acquired along the way or borrowed from their friends in order to display something white, even if it was only a white collar pinned to a blue sweater.

The rest of us stared curiously at them, smiled and made jokes about these touches of white, so utterly preposterous among the grimy surroundings. But soon we gave up for we became aware of the seriousness of what they were doing.

Some ships are eternally immobile, overgrown with seaweed, at the bottom of the sea. Others still proudly sail the waters above them. Meanwhile, these shipwrecked mariners, tossed by the storm on the hostile sands of a lifeless shore, are waiting. And as they wait they think of the past and the future, of the living and the dead. They take stock of themselves as well; at this moment they know that they are alive, and indeed that, at this very moment, they are living, not here but outside, under the flag which for so long flew above them.

Sight in the Sky

June 14

A fighter plane flies high overhead, leaving behind it a straight, narrow streak of white smoke, which stays in place, as if it were frozen, or like a line traced by a diamond across the glassy sky.

Fatality

June 16

Some Russian prisoners are working outside the enclosure, to re-enforce the barbed wire. Sitting on the ground, with the darkening sky behind them, they look more like ghosts than men.

They do not speak, and their gestures are fatalistically slow. Every now and then they all freeze at the same time into immobility, kneeling, crouching, or standing with upraised arm, as the case may be, for as long as five or ten minutes, like figures in a reel of film that has ceased unwinding. Forgetful of the fact that they are alive, they become the echo of a single gesture or position. They turn into memories of themselves.

Vaudeville

June 18

Sights of the day: the barley growing in the field at the east side of the camp has begun to turn golden yellow. Along the rough road between this field and the barbed-wire fence, a girl on a bicycle rides by, and meets the usual hunchbacked shepherd and his sheep. From inside the enclosure someone calls out "hello." The girl looks around, while the shepherd and his flock go indifferently their way. A clump of red flowers has blossomed between the two rows of fencing. A seagull flies across the stormy sky, like a handkerchief, carried away by the wind. Today is Monday. Tomorrow the program may be radically changed. There will be an old man on the bicycle instead of a girl, and the day will be Tuesday.

Northern Sky

June 20

For two months, now, I have been here, in the far north.

A few miraculously sunny days, and all the rest filled with rain and cold and wind, an angry wind that cards the clouds as if they were so much wool. There is ceaseless combat between white and black clouds in an unbounded, lowering sky.

I have never before seen a sky so wide, so overhanging. The earth is empty and flat like a slab of marble, and there is no obstacle to break the wide view. Only at the horizon does this plane cut the celestial sphere, so that anyone living here must feel as if he were under a great glass cone. Yet in spite of this immensity, he is in constant fear of being stifled, and even if he were a free man he would still feel like an imprisoned one.

Ransom Value of an Internee

June 25

The newspaper, *La Voce della Patria,* of June 12, 1944, says that the German command will grant anyone in Italy who captures or reports an enemy the release of one interned Italian soldier. If there is no one whose release he particularly wishes to obtain, he will be given a cash reward of two thousand liras.

June Rain

June 28

It is pouring rain; the camp is a sea of mud, and the dripping huts look like old boats rotting in some forgotten harbor. The shirts and shorts hung up to dry on a wire in front of the hut hang limp, like a charwoman's rags.

In these parts hanging up the laundry is a futile act of faith. The weather is just as unstable as the temper of the rags called men, who are supposed to be drying out after immersion in the purifying bath of sorrow. After a brief moment of calm, they have sunk into a mood of complaint and gloom, of doubt, fear and resentment. It is just as futile an act of faith to believe in their spiritual resurrection.

The rain has ceased, and men are streaming outdoors. The camp is studded with puddles, and in them is mirrored the hopeless failure of the Italian middle class, clad in rags and pettiness.

"The Stars We Wear . . ."

My uniform is in a state of progressive disintegration. The lining is in tatters, the bars on my shoulders have lost their gold plating and revealed their copper soul, the elbows are frayed, the trousers are spattered with patches, the soles of my boots are worn through and the uppers are scuffed like dried rubber; buttons sewn on with wire have ripped the buttonholes to pieces.

But there is only one thing for which I feel real concern: that the stars should remain firmly attached to my lapels. Every morning I test the screws and tighten them to the nth degree.

"The stars we wear . . ."

Although I am a sworn enemy of everything militaristic, those stars are screwed into my skin, and to lose them would be like losing a fragment of myself.

The fair lady symbolic of Italy, depicted on official parchments and sheepskins, carrying now a sword, now a hammer, displaying a coat-of-arms or a simple piece of machinery, never failed, in the old days, to wear a star. She wore it on her crown, if she had one, or on her bare forehead if she was an honest proletarian and had had not even the most modest headpiece to her name.

The originator of the new political order branded the star as "stupid," and took it out of the picture. But Italy without a star was never Italy to me. Now he has deprived even his Fascist soldiers of their star, and in so doing he has made them my foes.

"The stars we wear . . ."

For a century past, Italians have been victims of war, that plague which humanity strives to make more necessary and more incurable than ever. And when an

Italian soldier dies, his body may cling to the earth, but the stars fly away from his jacket and add two new gems to the sparkling firmament. Perhaps it is for this reason that ours is the starriest sky in the world.

"The stars we wear" do not stand simply for our "soldierly spirit." They represent the pains and sorrows of our fathers, brothers and sons. That is why I love them as if they were a part of me, and only wearing them will I return to my native land and sky.

Sunday

July 6

Ever since eleven o'clock this morning there has been heavy traffic in the stormy sky. Group after group of planes has flown over, heading in a southwesterly direction. And from the southwest there has come a continuous dull roar. Sitting on the sand, with my back against one of the huts, I look through the barbed-wire fence at the clouds on the horizon and listen to the echo of other men's war.

On the rough road running around the enclosure the usual hunchbacked shepherd and his sheep go by. His hump is wedge-shaped, and when he halts it seems to merge with one of the fence posts. A lamb tries to slip through the barbed wire; he is caught over there, in one corner, and bleats pitifully in his effort to get free. His bleating is like the voice of a child and reminds me of my son. I am overcome by despair because his call gives me an exact measure of my helplessness.

The roar of the airplane motors has ceased, and the horizon is mute once more. Nothing can be heard but the wind, as it blows in an icy sheet against the fence and carries the lamb's bleating farther away, making it even more pitiful than before.

Still Raining

July 10

It's still raining. A ray of sun is not so much God's gift to men but a concession which men make to God. Everything's in reverse. It rains all day long, and just before dusk the sun emerges, a watermelon-red disk against a coal-black sky, an impossible sort of sun, halfway between the Apocalypse and a colored postcard. Impossible like everything else in this barren place.

July 11

We are all stacked in our bunks, one beside, one over the other, like immigrants, packed, sardine style, in the hold of a ship.

Sitting on the edge of his upper-story bunk, with his head bumping against the ceiling, Arturo is playing his accordion. The bellows open like the pages of a book, and memories drop out of them like pressed flowers, suddenly made green by the music. There is a little of everything. The warm silence of a summer evening, the café under the trees, near the fountain, on the outskirts of the city, with its iron seats and round tables. The furnished room on the top floor, the portable phonograph, which winds a skein of illusions on the shiny, revolving record.

Late evening melancholy, when we were ill fed, ill clad, but our hearts were full of riches and our heads swimming with dreams of glory, and we looked down at the rushing waters of the stream that ran like liquid black night under the bridge arches.

Night-time, looking from the shore of the stream at the train passing over the embankment. In the distance, the phosphorescent city, the red lights of the sign of the hotel beside the station and the echo of the band playing for outdoor dancing. On the opposite shore, close to the water, the "Red Barn," which whispers many a tale of drowning to the water. The dry warmth of a slender hand, in the dampness hanging like fog over the meadow. The nickel parts of the bicycle lying in the wet grass, that gleam like motionless fireflies in the dark.

Pacing up and down the empty avenues in bittersweet, vain expectation. Thinking voluptuously of death, counting the seconds for fear of losing a single one, with eyes burning. Snow in the suburbs. The factory win-

dows are all dark and ghosts look out from the icy trans-
parency of the glass. Standing with wet feet under the
lamppost, with the small circle of light like a bubble
against the pitch blackness.

The icy drops clinging to the lapels of her fur coat
(a drop on every single strand of fur), as I plunge my
face into them as if into a bed of dewy grass. Her warm
mouth, and the fragrance of her lipstick left on mine.

Arturo is turning the pages of every man's life story.
Every song is a picture from out of the past, and the hut
is filled with youth.

Contemporary Poetry

July 12

Hut No. 67, Room No. 12. Lieutenant Gianrico Te-
deschi is reading contemporary poets: Quasimodo, Mon-
tale, Ungaretti, Saba, Scipione, Cardarelli, Dora Mar-
tius, Rebora. The last-named is present not only in spirit
but also in body.

Here everything is different, and contemporary poets
speak in a new voice to Giovannino. Once upon a time
their voices were strange to his ears; he felt as if they
were almost hostile in their armor of ambiguity. They
were literary figures rather than human beings, somewhat like De Chirico's *Disconcerting Muses*.

But here they seem to speak straight from the heart. Their verses adhere to his sensibility as wet paper to a sheet of glass; the words are human and transparent, in them is repeated the eternal miracle of poetry, for they are extraordinarily applicable to the present situation.

Ungaretti and the desperate monotony of our days:

> *Once upon a time*
> *I did not know*
> *that even*
> *the evening conflagration*
> *of the sky*
> *was something*
> *quite ordinary*

Vittorio Sereni and the regret for times that can never return:

> *The cooling hour will come at last,*
> *with the wind that blows up over the dockyards*
> *of the canals, and the sky*
> *that retreats from the shore.*
> *Will you, too, return, Diana,*
> *among the tables spread outside*
> *and the people intent upon their drinks,*
> *under the distant moon?*
> *An orchestra is softly playing*
> *to the quivering air . . .*

Rebora, the so-called hermetic poet, and the theme of homesickness:

In our veins there migrates the misty
plain, where before a deliberate gaze
Milan emerges in the distance,
repeating a corroded forehead
in monotonous ecstasies
from the familiar façades.
The old air, note it well, cuts decisively
along outstretching streets
the sorrow which accompanies
torrents of winter water . . .

The rooftops of Milanese houses
guide the serene heartbeat
which has narrowly escaped the marks of death.
Still untouched is the forehead of a world
rich in pity the length of its muffled walls,
while on squares and avenues
the weather moves a reproach
like the cutting wind
from the Lombard lakes and from the remote
reflowering astral air.

The familiar cadence of the local dialect
the misty, perplexed outskirts
stretching toward a distant perfection of trees
our footsteps on the avenues.

Who invented the word "hermetical"? Who launched
this slander?

Notes

Ghosts lurk, by night, at every corner of the huts.

*   *   *

In the dark room an accordion is playing. We lie in our bunks, one beside, one over the other. The ghosts, summoned by the music, come and sit down on the benches around the table.

*   *   *

Every morning, when I wake up, I look at the picture of my little Carlotta. Sometimes she seems to smile, at other times she is angry. At once I can say: "Today I'm in a good mood," or "Today I'm in a bad mood." For our eyes see what we want them to see.

*   *   *

The big huts, where two hundred and eighty men sleep in bunks at three different levels, with their ragged clothes and other belongings hanging from the ceiling, and with noisy individuals milling about the stoves and tables below, are reminiscent of gold rush miners' cabins, which were stores, taverns, bars and dancehalls as well. From one minute to the next it seems as if a dancing girl might start pirouetting on one of the tables, or a pistol go off and an arrow whistle by and imbed itself, quivering, in the wall. Of course, nothing like this happens. The men around the tables are weighing potato rations as carefully as if they were gold.

*   *   *

Roll call. A blast of the bugle, and here are six thousand men, standing mute and motionless before the silence of the empty huts. When I am standing in line and the bugle calls me to attention, my personality is completely lost and I am only an infinitesimal part of collective impotency, like one brick in a high wall. Amid this deathly immobility something dreadful is about to happen. My little boy runs out from behind one of the huts, and a man runs after him with intent to kill. He catches sight of me and calls for help. But I am a brick in the wall, and my heart is a live insect shut up in a diamond.

The "at ease" signal has been given. I am surprised to find that I can still move and talk.

*   *   *

"How shall we sing the Lord's song in a strange land?" —Psalm 137.4

Younger Generation

There is poison in their hearts. Once upon a time they vented their bitterness in the papers of the Fascist student organization. Now they turn the same arguments against Fascism, but in ambiguous terms, because they are too wary to commit themselves. They are getting ready to turn their internment experience to profit, to make a place for themselves on new newspapers and to vent the bitterness they feel over their failure.

Moral Support

July 24

There is a change in the tone of certain letters from home. Captain P. has just received one that says:

"We are proud of your strength of character and appreciate the nobility of the sacrifice you are making. Good for you! Hold fast!"

Whereas in all the preceding letters his family had written:

"Don't be a fool. Come on back to Italy, whatever the cost. Just swim with the current."

The last letter—the first quoted above—was dated June 6. Strange coincidence: on this same day the Allies captured Rome and landed in Normandy.

Straws in the Wind

July 26

When Captain L. took his knapsack down from the wall
he saw something that he had never noticed before. On
the white cardboard tag, there was a pencil drawing by
an unknown English prisoner: a horse's head framed by
a horseshoe and the two printed words: GOOD LUCK.

In a recently arrived package from Italy Lieutenant
F. discovered, inside a bag of sugar, a 12.5 cartridge, obviously the gift of an English flyer who had shot up the
train while it was on its way hither. The new alliance
with England is beginning to bear fruit.

The Shadow

Once upon a time there was my shadow. It was a bit of
myself, clad in black velvet, that I took with me everywhere I happened to go. It went faithfully along, just
ahead or behind, or even under my feet, according to
the hour, day and season.

Sometimes my shadow was not alone; it led another
bit of myself that walked beside me, holding my hand
and warming my heart.

Once upon a time there was my shadow, but those
were the days when children were made of flesh and

blood and not of refrigerated memories, when the sun in the sky was a real sun and shadows could live in it, whereas in this northern mist they fade and die.

The Father

Once upon a time there was a father, a gentleman endowed with great dignity, a conspicuous mustache and experience of the world and its ways.

He was always saying that in his younger days boys didn't smoke or drink or go out dancing; they didn't play cards, ask for new suits and pocket money or wear out the heels of their shoes. They never raced about in cars or stuffed themselves with a giant pizza, or wasted their time with movies and comics; they never lit matches by scraping them on the wall or left dirty water in the bathtub, or wore out the seats of their trousers or went out bareheaded or kept their bedroom light on until two o'clock in the morning. They took no interest in skiing or motor-scootering, they didn't have to send all their letters by airmail or track mud into the house or ask what there was to eat.

And this respectable father said loftily that no honest man would soil his hands in politics. The thing to do was to follow the general trend, to observe the law, to obey orders without discussion, to shy away from responsibility and generally keep out of hot water.

His sons esteemed his advice to be pure gold. And so they ended up behind a barbed-wire fence, where they had no choice but to be just as virtuous as the boys their father said he used to know when he was young. They don't smoke, dance, go to the movies or stuff themselves, and so on, and so on.

But, Father, if they ever come home! . . .

Boredom

August 3

This endless boredom is like an unrelenting noose around the neck. The misery of having nothing to look forward to, the comfortless melancholy of every hour of the day and night. . . . During the last two months the outside world has witnessed one important event after another, but here the repercussion has been no more than that obtained by throwing stones into a muddy pond: a momentary ripple, and then everything returns to the same deadliness as before. Futile days, hours that are swallowed up, one after another, like the links of a chain lowered into the water, one pulling the next after it. And I look on at the process, in anguished impotence, as if I were seeing the blood fall, drop by drop, from an open vein in my wrist onto the silently absorbent sand.

In this sand the hours of my life are obliterated, every one robbing me of a drop of the stuff of life, of the smiles of my children. I can see myself going, step by step, down stairs which can never be climbed again. This state of inanition is sticky and coagulative, like the hot August weather. The most world-shaking events fail to stir it. The day must be near when they'll say the war's over, but I shan't even care; the good news will fall upon me as a stone into a muddy pond. A man can be deadened by dreaming too much, by letting his desires fly too high over the limits of reality.

Vincenzo Romeo

August 8

Those flies on his white face. They crawl over his lowered eyelids, close to the nostrils, between the half-open lips. You are made aware of the presence of death not so much by the fact that the flies arouse no reaction from his face, but rather because they seem so completely extraneous to you. If flies were to crawl over the face of a live man, even one deep in sleep, you would feel them on your own skin as well, whereas now they seem to be crawling over a rock or a marble-topped table, in short, over some inanimate thing. All the living are bound by imperceptible radiations, like threads, together, and in death the threads are broken.

The body is laid out on four packing cases in a sort of a storeroom, occupied by several unmade beds, in the infirmary. Yes, he is like an inanimate object, with a ragged overcoat thrown over his body and a band wound around his head to prevent the jaw from sagging.

Four fellow-officers are keeping watch and they too seem so absent from the land of the living that it is hard to imagine them walking and talking again. Others have come to pay their respects, and after lining up in the corridor they go away as silently as they came, as if their only purpose had been to assure themselves that he was really dead. It seems quite impossible. Half an hour ago he was washing himself at the pump and now he is gone.

The pump is fifteen feet or so distant from the watch-tower, and behind it a hundred men were standing in line with basins and pitchers. One of them put his basin, filled with water, down on the sand, six feet away from the barbed-wire fence, and prepared to wash. It was a warm, sunny morning, under an unusually blue sky. A sudden bang stopped the buzz of conversation. Everyone looked first at the body lying on the sand and then at the watchtower almost directly above. The sentry, a little man wearing round eyeglasses and an old-fashioned helmet, with protruding sidepieces, emerged from his post like a horned snake out of a basket and looked with an air of utter indifference at the quick death agony.

When the other men understood what had happened, they cried out in impotent rage. The bullet had rebounded from one of the victim's bones, struck the corner of a nearby hut, gone through a military jacket and a soup bowl and finally stayed its fury in a pile of blankets.

The sentry had "cased" his man. He saw him put the basin on the ground and, with gun in hand, watched his every subsequent movement. When the prisoner, bending over the basin, raised his arm to hang his towel on the fence the sentry fired. The prisoner's hand had not yet touched the wire when the bullet brought him down.

He died on the spot, twelve or thirteen feet from the tower, and his blood was absorbed by the dry sand. When the man in the tower saw that the body had stiffened he picked up the telephone and reported to the guardroom: "I've killed an Italian." Of course, he'll be punished. If a sentry shoots by mistake, he's put under arrest; if he kills, he's discharged. It's all provided for in army regulations.

Soon afterward the air abruptly darkened. A storm blew up, seeming to signify divine displeasure, and we all stood at the windows, waiting for lightning to strike the tower. But the storm came to an end before anything happened; the Almighty Judge had merely entered a formal protest. As for the blood on the sand, the rain washed it away.

Operators

August 10

On the latrine doors there are all sorts of notices and signs.

Exchange Divine Comedy and pound of rice for ciga-
rettes. Captain X., Hut Y.

Flavor your food! One ounce of best Greek pepper,
exchange for tobacco. Lieutenant Y. Hut Z.

Expert repairs watches, exchanges food for cheap,
hopelessly broken timepieces in order to obtain spare
parts for repairs. Captain C., Hut Y.

Exchange form letter and parcel-request card for
bread and cigarettes.

German grammar and razor blades, exchange for Eng-
lish grammar and new toothbrush.

Big business operations! In front of the latrine door,
Russian prisoners are pumping out the contents of the
cesspool into a wagon. Every time the guard looks the
other way they hurriedly trade cigarettes for camp
money, with Italian officers who seem to be strolling indifferently by.

Just inside, a Russian as filthy and wretched as the
very incarnation of Siberia sits with his trousers down
on one of the cheap wooden seats, in the process of relieving himself. Before him a group of Italian officers
are gesticulating. Finally the Russian extracts from the
greasy depths of his trouser pockets a slice of bread,
which he holds out in his right hand, while the left
takes their money.

On the Sand

Naked men, bundles of pale skin, sunbathing between one hut and another. One, two, three thousand of them, like white worms on the ground.

But the scene has nothing of a summer resort about it, in spite of the sandy ground and the illusory feeling that the sea lies there, beyond the barbed-wire fence, where actually an endless plain stretches all the way to the horizon. No, it is more like the *Lazzaretto,* the hospital for contagious diseases in Milan, this total immobility of the stagnant, oppressive air, this sun so hot that it seems as if it must melt in the sky, this expectation of a storm which will wash the plague away.

Northern Sun

We lie flat on our backs on a canvas stretched over the sand, which is black and greasy to the touch, because here even the earth is redolent of machinery and coal. We are naked, with towels wrapped around our heads and over our eyes, so that the only way we can see the dazzling sun is by squinting through the cloth. As the sun's rays filter through the weave, they are refracted on the white threads and make all the colors of the rainbow. Herein is our only real pleasure, for this sun warms only the skin, and leaves heart and bones just as cold as they were before. It's an *ersatz* sun, strictly for propaganda purposes.

Maurice

Maurice Chevalier is dead.* Someone shot at General de Gaulle with a machine gun hidden under the high altar of the cathedral of Notre Dame. The general was not hurt, but, out of the surrounding crowd the bullet intended for him hit Chevalier instead.

I remember, years ago, when Dempsey defeated Carpentier, and it seemed to me that not only the national hero, Georges, but the whole French nation had been KO'd in the ring. Now that Chevalier is gone, I feel as if France were dead. When I used to play "Prosper" or *"Ma pomme"* on the phonograph, I could see Maurice cavort on the turning record, with his wide-as-Paris smile, and my thoughts wandered to Napoleon and the Merry Widow, to the Académie Française and the Three Musketeers, to Murat and *Boule de Suif,* to *La Bohème* and the Moulin Rouge and the Foreign Legion. There is a France that all of us Italians have in our blood, and if our hearts beat faster to the strains of the *"Marseillaise,"* it is because this is, in a way, our anthem, just as Paris is our capital city. Chevalier was the voice and the smile of this France, and now he is gone from us, taking a part of them with him.

---

* Maurice Chevalier is alive and flourishing. But in the internment camp we were given news that he was dead.

General de Gaulle is safe, and Chevalier is dead. I could almost wish it were the other way around. . . . God forgive me, I know nothing about politics. I suffered the pains of hell, when in order to make way for a huge new stadium, the Fascists tore down half a dozen decayed nineteenth-century houses, inhabited only by ghosts.

Autumn Evening

I look at my dried hands and bony wrists and feel very sorry for myself. Under the sixty pounds of weight I have lost there was something I considered long since dead. My spirit was submerged in fat, but now it is so crystal clear that I can mirror myself in it and rediscover an image of my distant youth. When I look at my small bones, I feel the same consuming anxiety as I feel for the frailty of my son. In short, I begin to regard myself with love.

Just now I'm hungry to the point of weakness. My illness prevents me from eating any of the camp rations, except the slippery, tasteless potatoes. I am alone in the hut, and there is a knapsack full of food at my feet, brought by some new arrival. In the sultry air of the August evening I am so completely lost in my thoughts that I hardly see a gaunt hand searching the knapsack. I say and do nothing; I allow the thin fingers to grasp a piece of white bread.

Then I mingle with the hundreds of men walking up
and down the length of the barbed-wire fence, and
munch the bread along the way. The searchlights which
circle around from the tower and periodically fall upon
me seem to be ferreting out my guilt. My heart skips
a beat, but I am not too deeply upset; in fact I am
happy. My son was hungry and I let him steal a piece of
bread.

"I'm my own son, really," I reflect. And I feel as if I
were under my own protection.

Chee

August 30

Giovannino is sitting on the deserted sand. He is alone,
and yet he is not alone. He had three children, but one
of them never enjoyed so much as a ray of light or a
breath of air or a name, for death already held him in
its icy grasp when he was born.

But Giovannino breathed into his mouth, gave him
some of the light of his own eyes and made a name for
him out of a fragment of his own heart: Chee. So it is
that the unborn Chee lived. He stayed close to his
father, and there he is now, although nobody knows it.

For his other children, time passes; they grow older
by the minute. But for Chee there is no time, and he
prolongs the youth of his father. Giovannino has three

children: two of them sweeten his life, but Chee reconciles him to death.

*   *   *

Men have separated Giovannino from his other children, but Chee they cannot take away, even in death. For on the day when Giovannino shuffles off this mortal coil, Chee will still be beside him. He will take his father's hand, and together they will walk over the dark clouds and stormy seas of Eternity.

Chee is a bird that has built his nest in Giovannino's heart. For three years he has warmed Chee with his love; the pale skin is rosy, the eyes shine like two black pearls and the head is covered with black ringlets. He has made him a long white nightshirt and Chee, even without height or weight, looks like a Christmas card angel. Chee doesn't know how to talk, but he understands his father. He is a segment of his father's heart and lives on its beating.

*   *   *

Giovannino sits on the deserted sand, at the far end of the camp, apparently alone. But all the time Chee is perched on his right shoulder, leaning his face against his father's thin cheek. Together they look beyond the fence and beyond life itself, as if they were waiting for something.

The Smashed Food Parcel

Today I received a parcel from home.

At this point of our story, let us look back at the moment when Signora 3432.5 (I'm No. 6865, and she's my better half, isn't she?), who knew me in my carefree bachelor days, has joyfully finished wrapping a food parcel addressed to the father of her numerous Albertino and Carlotta.

"There," the good woman says to herself. "The package is ready to go. The Minister of Communications will telephone the Postmaster General and say: 'Look out for the food parcel that's on the way to Signor Giovannino. I want to be sure that it's treated with the proper consideration.' 'Of course,' the Postmaster will reply. 'I've already fired the clerk that canceled the stamps without asking permission. Everything's taken care of.' "

These, then, are the circumstances under which the parcel leaves the postoffice. It doesn't travel in a mail truck, but in the arms of a trusted employee, reposing on a purple cushion. "Dark blue would set it off better," says the sender, and in a trice the purple cushion is set aside in favor of a dark blue one.

"Here's Signor Giovannino's food parcel," announces the trusted employee, when he comes to the railway station.

"Signor Giovannino, did you say?" echoes the station-master. "I'll not lose a minute." And he runs to the

telephone. "Attention! Food parcel for Signor Gio-
vannino! Put a special car on No. 334. It's already gone?
Then hook it on at Bologna. What, Bologna's gone too?
Well, do *some*thing about it!"

And so the parcel is on its way, enjoying sole occu-
pancy of a first-class compartment and reposing on a
blue cushion. Travelers waiting on the various station
platforms pay it their respects as the special train goes
by. "Hats off!" shouts a veteran of the Risorgimento to
a youth corrupted by American movies and syncopation.
"Hat's off, when your country's parcel passes by!"

(The Wife is thrilled by this scene. Time to teach that
youth a lesson! And, sure enough, a husky porter gives
him a kick in the pants. Well, he had it coming to him!)

The trip continues. Now we are somewhere in Germany.

"Das Paket des Herrn Giovanninen!" they telephone
to the camp. And they inquire whether it should be
sent on via ordinary channels, that is, on a truck.

"Are you crazy?"

And so a taxi brings the honorable food parcel all the
way to the internment camp, where a brief but poignant
ceremony accompanies its delivery to the addressee. Giovannino, dinner is ready!

*   *   *

This is how Giovannino's better half must have
imagined a food parcel's story. There's no other explanation of the way she chose to pack it, in a box made
of paper-thin plywood, held together by nails symboli-

cal of a fierce desire for national unity, even against God's will.

Let us admit that, if the parcel *had* traveled according to the Wife's desire, it would have reached its destination undamaged. That is, if the lid had stood up under the impact of the address sticker. But since, in reality, things went very differently, the object I have just received is not so much a proper food parcel as a sack, containing the remains of what was originally one of the most phenomenal packages in all history.

If I had said simply that today I received a smashed food parcel, I should be at exactly the same point as I was at the beginning of my story, and I should have saved several hundred superfluous words in the bargain. But what do you expect? Literature is like that, and so is politics, for that matter.

* * *

And so today I received a smashed food parcel. (Please overlook the fact that I have switched to the past tense. The whole thing is so distressing that I am trying to push it as far away as I can.) I took it at once to Talotti's room and dumped the contents out onto the table. Nobody was there but soon Talotti returned. He stood at the door, lighting his pipe, and said sorrowfully:

"If I so much as step out of the door, someone's sure to play some crude trick on me. Who is the unsavory creature that has littered my table with garbage?"

"What do you mean, garbage?" muttered Schenardi. "Can't you see that's our daily ration of peat?"

"Peat, my eye!" exclaimed Coppola. "That's sliced turnips! Nowadays they serve them without benefit of table silver."

"Excuse me," I put in. "That's my food parcel. What you mistook for sliced turnips is excelsior, soaked in cocoa and butter. When you sprinkle cocoa over the contents of various broken jars, bags and cardboard boxes, not to mention the excelsior, splintered plywood and other packing material, then the general effect is that of peat or garbage, as you will."

A moment of perfect quiet followed. Then I went over to the table and extracted from the mess a scrap of something white, which turned out to be the list of the parcel's original contents, whatever they might be. From it I read out loud:

"Jam, butter, honey, cocoa, rice, flour, tobacco, sugar, insect powder, Parmesan cheese, soap."

"A splendid assortment!" said Talotti, in the calm voice and manner of a Venetian gentleman.

"Let's see if anything's missing," said Schenardi, injecting a practical note characteristic of his native Liguria.

"I'm going for a few minutes to No. 31, where there's a Neapolitan meeting," called Coppola over one shoulder. "I'll be back soon to give you a hand."

"If I hang around much longer, I'll simply pick up that mess and chuck it into the stove," I said. And with that I went away.

When I came back Coppola was playing some of his own excellent musical compositions on the accordion.

Talotti had ensconced himself comfortably in his bunk to smoke his pipe while Schenardi, covered with dirt and sweat, was putting the last touches on the job of salvaging the parcel.

"Almost everything's here," he said. "The only things I can't find are the honey and the insect powder."

Rice, cocoa, flour and sugar had all been mixed together but, with the aid of an improvised sieve, he had separated the rice from the rest. As for the cocoa, flour and sugar, he had put them in water, in order that any particles of dust and scraps of paper should come to the surface. After that, with the addition of some evaporated milk and a few minutes of cooking, he hoped to produce a first-rate chocolate pudding.

Talotti and I showered him with compliments and dubbed him on the spot "Treasure-hunter." Only Coppola continued to call him "Maria," because of his proven culinary and housekeeping ability, but even he was sufficiently carried away to put in a good word for Schenardi's famous checked flannel cowboy's shirt. This had been sent to our first camp, in Poland, by Schenardi's fiancée, with a note which said: "You can use this for skiing. Shall I send skiis too, or are they provided by the management of the hotel?"

That evening we feasted. While the water in which the rice was cooking won a series of defensive victories against the pervasive odor of the peat in the stove below, we decided, somewhat illogically, to sample the jam. Coppola, the musician, led the way. He spread some jam on a slice of bread, bit into it and then unexpectedly leaped to his feet and dashed out of the room like a Bach fugue. A moment of confusion followed, until Schenardi had studied the remaining half of the slice of bread and announced: "There are traces of honey and insect powder. In fact, the present contents of the jam jar might be called insecticidal honey. Our mistake is natural enough, because the mixture has the color of apricot jam."

"And what about the jam that was in the parcel in the first place?" Talotti asked calmly.

Schenardi started searching among the débris heaped up in one corner of the room, but without success. He went to wash his hands at the pump, but when he came back they were stickier than before. However, there was a beaming expression on his face.

"The jam's accounted for, too," he announced triumphantly. "This cube isn't soap, as we imagined; it's solid jam that has dried up in transit. It was coated with butter, and that is what gave it the shiny look and greasy feel which made us take it for soap."

"What about the real soap, then?" asked Coppola, who came back just as we were throwing the false soap away. But we did not pause to look for it. The rice was cooked to a turn, and we had need to console ourselves for the disappointments we had suffered thus far. As usual, Coppola was the first to lift a forkful of steaming rice to his mouth. He swallowed it and then made a wry face.

"It stinks of tobacco," he protested.

"Oh, very faintly," I assured him. "A couple of spoon-fuls of grated cheese will put that straight."

We sprinkled the rice abundantly with cheese. But this time the musician was more cautious and waited for the rest of us to begin, meanwhile thoroughly stir-ring the two ingredients of the dish together. Little by little, our imaginations were stirred by the sight of a white foam rising over the rice.

"That accounts for the soap," said Schenardi after a quick analysis of the supposed Parmesan cheese. The cheese had been removed, in a crumbled condition, from the parcel, but while some of the crumbs were really cheese, others were fragments of excellent white laundry soap.

"Very good!" exclaimed Coppola ironically. "So every-thing was there, eh?"

But Talotti had sufficient wit and grace to dispel our embarrassment.

"Let's have a good smoke and forget all about it," he suggested.

We lit our pipes and inhaled deeply. A moment later the room was smoking like a fish-and-chips shop. Even Talotti threw his pipe out the window and sputtered in frankly vulgar terms. Do not be surprised at this reaction on the part of a perfect gentleman, who is also my very good friend. Have you ever tried smoking tobacco mixed with butter?

We still had in our possession the ingredients of a pudding. But Schenardi was prudently engaged in letter-

ing a sign: DELICIOUS CHOCOLATE PUDDING; WILL EX-
CHANGE FOR TWO CIGARETTES.

*   *   *

And so today I received a smashed food parcel. I'm
glad, even if at the end nothing was left except a dirty
piece of cardboard. I washed it off and, all of a sudden,
like the moon peeking out from behind a cloud, there
was a chubby round face. The first photograph of Carlotta.

Why shouldn't I be happy, when I had received the
most wonderful parcel in the world?

What a Youngish Man
Can't Help Thinking

September 3

He had cleaned up his "castle," detached the boards, run
a lighted match along the interstices, washed the frame
of the bunk with a chloride solution, stopped up the
cracks with tar stolen from the men who fixed the roof,
thrown away the straw mattress and adapted himself to
sleeping on bare wood, but the lice were more aggressive this last night than ever before. Over and over, he
woke up with itching neck and wrists, and lit a dozen
sulphur matches in vain. These disgusting bugs are un-
cannily clever at hiding themselves, and the myriad

cracks in the wooden walls afford them plenty of oppor-
tunity to do so.

He is thinking how, just lately, Churchill said again
that Italy had lost the war and would have to pay, a fact
which apparently many people have forgotten. We shall
pay, sir; don't worry, we shall pay.

He is thinking, too, of the razed cities, of the hatreds
aroused among his own people: the Black Brigades, the
Patriots, the Republicans, the supporters of Badoglio,
the Monarchists. . . . Of the words which Mussolini addressed to Italian Fascist battalions training in Germany: "When you return to Italy, don't hesitate to fight
against those of your fellow-citizens who are irrespon-
sible or traitors as the case may be. . . ."

Yes, we must pay, pay to the full. Even at the cost of
retrogression, everyone must limit his needs. Everyone
must work. But for whom? For what? What is the national economy? Who is to run the railroads? Who is to
pay retired schoolteachers' pensions? Of course, there
are many things one can do without. That is something
he has learned in internment. Besides, it's only a matter
of surviving for a few years; then everything will find a
natural solution. If there is no peace on earth, there is
plenty of peace below it, and a place in the shade for all
and sundry.

But will those people who were most spoiled in the
past be capable of sacrifice and privation? The middle
class has gone to pieces, the "ruling class" has been submerged by its own inertia. The common people, of
course, but who are they? Those who, on July 26, 1943,

after the arrest of Mussolini, demonstrated on the streets, raising red flags beside the Italian tricolor, along with pictures of Badoglio, Mazzini, Lenin, Garibaldi, Stalin and Matteotti? Who called upon tobacconists to destroy postage and tax stamps, simply because they bore the Fascist emblem upon them?

He is thinking of pitiless England, of casually murderous America. . . .

And what about Russia? Communism exercises a tremendous pull. But isn't it just another totalitarian "ism"?

And Christianity, then? But Christianity spills over, all too easily, into politics. There are plenty of politicians who want to make Jesus Christ into a political leader.

Socialism? Liberalism? Do we want to put on the tattered garb of our fathers, who are responsible for the mess in which we find ourselves today?

With all these thoughts in his mind, he tosses on his hard wooden bunk, while hunger, lice and discouragement assail him. Lying there in the darkness, he feels as if he were laid away in the tomb, dead beyond all hope of resurrection. He gets up and goes to look outside. It is a perfect summer night, with a full moon and the stars neatly divided into constellations. Suddenly, toward the west, there are flashing lights, like fireflies. Then searchlights play on the sky, motors hum and guns roar in reply. They are bombing Bremen; perhaps these are the same planes that have raided Italian cities as well. His tragedy and the enemy's tragedy are one. But all he can do is go back to bed and scratch his neck, as angrily as if it belonged on someone else's shoulders.

He feels as if he couldn't endure it any longer.

"I'm sick and tired of having to be an Italian!"

New Worlds

September 7

Here everything is seen as if through a magnifying glass: a blade of grass, a hair, a particle of dust. Having lost one world, these prisoners must create another, within the few square feet of sand to which they are confined, and people it with their everyday discoveries. The smallest objects loom up large to the dispossessed, just as the least action takes on importance amid their total inanition.

When they are nauseated by sterile hankering for the dead past, they turn desperately to the slightest clue to the future. A Russian, a cloud in the sky, a lark, a ray of sun, the cancellation mark on a postcard, the color of the watchtower in the setting sun, any of these things is enough to convince them that they still belong to the world of the living. They fancy that they are discovering something and all the while they are creating it, day by day, out of material from their past. It is no new world, but rather a very old world, all their own. What they are discovering is their self.

If any internee fails to observe the details around him, it can only be because inside the prison of his bones he has only organs of respiration, circulation, digestion, elimination, etc. And for this reason he is sensitive only to hunger, thirst, heat, cold and homesickness.

Monotony

September 15

Time marches on, but in this desert twenty-four of its hours are as sluggish as water swept from the banks of a river into a stagnant pool. Eventually the water moves on, but in the river it is alive, while here it is dead.

Dead hours circle slowly, under an opaque glass shell. Perhaps some day the glass will crack, and time will pull back into its orbit these drifting hours and these drifting men.

Giovannino

September 18

Prisoners, reclining on the triangle of grass on the mound directly below the watchtower, press the blades of a pair of scissors against their eyes, as if in a children's game. Between the blades they frame distant objects, which stand out in relief against the rays of the setting sun. They imagine cutting the wires of the enclosing fence, one by one. But then, of course, the sentry would shoot them down. . . .

Giovannino is thirty-six years old, with a wife and children at loose ends, in another area of the world-shaking tragedy. And here he is, amusing himself with a pair of scissors. How very young you are, old man Giovannino!

A Friend

September 30

I came across a stone in front of the door of the hut and took it for a walk around the camp, kicking it just ahead of me with my big toe.

Tomorrow at three o'clock I have an appointment to go for another walk with the same stone, which I left in a hole, within easy reach of the door. We get on very well together.

A Parcel for Papa

"We must get to work on a parcel for Papa," says Signora Margherita. "The postcard came today."

Signor Luigi looks up from his newspaper, Signora Flaminia lays down her book and Albertino puts aside his efforts to achieve an education. Only Carlotta shows a total lack of interest as she struggles to cover the minutes that separate her from her arrival at the venerable age of half a year.

*   *   *

"Let's begin with some cookies," says Signora Flaminia, starting to take them out of the cake box. But Signora Margherita has a word to say:

"Go slow, there! I have an idea he doesn't want them any more."

None of them is quite sure, and so they get out the dozen letters in which there is mention of a food parcel.

"While we're at it, we may as well see what he says about other things to eat," suggests Signor Luigi.

And because he is a good organizer, he sets forth a definite plan. The two women are to look over the letters, while he draws up a list of all the foodstuffs mentioned and the exact remark which has been made about each one. Signora Flaminia and Signora Margherita proceed to read aloud every reference to cookies, and Signor Luigi jots them all down. Three quarters of an hour later, they have the cooky story complete.

"Cookies not advisable."
"Cookies always welcome."
"Cookies, if you think they're a good idea."
"Yes, cookies."

"Cookies not wanted."
"Omit cookies."
"Not so sure about cookies."
"No cookies, please."
"More cookies, if you don't mind."
"Not so many cookies, after all."
"Cookies serve no purpose."
"Cookies delicious."
"Cookies stupid."

Signor Luigi counts the votes. *Pro,* five (because "not so many" signifies that some are still wanted); *con,* six; *neutral,* two ("if you think they're a good idea," "not so sure").

"Six to five, in favor of the negative," he announces.

Signora Margherita has some doubts, of a strictly mathematical variety. Six plus five plus two make thirteen. And there are only twelve letters.

* * *

Once, twice, three times the list is checked. The letters are read, word by word, several times over. After forty-five more minutes it is concluded that the phrase "cookies stupid" is a malicious interpolation. In no other letter is there any reference to the brainpower of a cookie. Which one of the two women is guilty of slipping it in? The discussion drags on for some time, until a sudden ray of light falls upon it. The interpolation was an unsolicited two cents' worth put in by Albertino.

* * *

The revised vote is now ready for scrutiny. Five *pros*, five *cons* and two *neutrals*. Things are at the same point as before. Perplexity reigns, but Signora Margherita has a sudden inspiration.

"We didn't take account of the dates. The last letter is the one that should decide it."

The letters are hastily put into chronological order. The last one contains the remark: "Cookies, if you think they're a good idea." And the next to the last: "Not so sure about cookies."

Well, why not leave the question undecided for the time being and go on to the next item on the list, which happens to be butter? But after due consideration, it seems wise to leave butter in suspense also. And so on, all the way down. At the end of the whole process, there is nothing in the future food parcel but one small cake of chocolate. There can be no doubt that the recipient really wants it.

But now Carlotta is surprised with the form postcard in her tiny, murderous hands. And only in return for the cake of chocolate will she hand it over.

*   *   *

Darkness has fallen. Signora Margherita is in tears, old Signora Flaminia is groaning and sighing, and Signor Luigi, after a statement to the effect that the young men of today don't even know how to be prisoners of war, has gone outside to talk to the dog about times gone by.

Sitting in a dark corner, Albertino takes advantage of the state of emergency to unwrap the piece of candy he has kept for a whole week in his overall pocket in order to slip it into his father's food parcel. Very slowly, he unwinds the paper and gives the candy a tiny lick. Then he winds it up again. Yesterday he gave it a lick too, and the day before, and three days before, as well. The candy has shrunk in size, and the paper is wrinkled from repeated wrapping and unwrapping. But his father won't care; he'll understand. After all, his father is a man of the world! . . .

* * *

The Angelus has rung. Signora Margherita comes out of her melancholy torpor and rebels against the slowness of the project. Leaping to her feet, she sweeps everything off the table and into the box. Without even looking, she presses it down with her fists. Albertino has barely time to give one last lick to the candy. A few swift blows of the hammer, and the cover is nailed down securely. Total packing time: four minutes flat.

* * *

A few months later, when Giovannino opens the parcel, he finds the contents very touching.

"How lovingly they put it together! There's a little of everything. An iron to press my clothes, Mother's glasses and Father's old wallet, just to be sure I won't forget them. That's a parcel with a purpose!"

Madhouse

October 6

Here everything is intensified to the nth degree. Homesickness turns into despair, inactivity into inertia, poverty is misery and desire is frenzy. Faith becomes a mania and, as soon as a chaplain appears, a crowd of internees assails him. They press in on him from every side, push him into a corner and overwhelm him with an account of their sins.

Every corner is a confessional. An hour before reveille, the chapel is filled with men praying and singing psalms, and in the hall a whole long line waits to receive communion.

The exchange of clothes and food, a natural enough phenomenon under circumstances like these, is a full-fledged business, with a market place, price quotations, agents and advertising. The simplest manual activity is considered heavy industry and the latrine door is covered with want ads.

Has your watch stopped? D., in Hut No. 23-B, is at your service. Unbreakable crystals in all sizes.

Leather watch-straps, book-binding. Hut No. 23-A, next to last hall.

Parcel recipients! Hot-air stoves, inexpensive. Exchanged for food and cigarettes. Hut No. 89, Room 4.

Yes, everything is overdone.

The lectures, which started out in such a praiseworthy fashion, have turned into oratorical orgies. There are five or ten of them every evening. In whatever hut you choose to visit after eight P.M. you are sure to find someone standing on a table to harangue his fellows. Music, poetry, science, political economy, history, philosophy, drama, films, vaudeville, literature, chemistry, religion, high finance. Today Lieutenant B gave a good, solid talk on humor. Others, too, have spoken on subjects with which they are actually acquainted. But all too often, the lecturers are simply individuals who no sooner see an empty table than they jump up and start rattling on about the first thing that comes into their minds. Probably they are making up for having kept silence or discreetly whispered during the twenty years of dictatorship just past.

News from Abroad

October 10

"Albertino is tired of waiting. Every now and then he sits down at his desk and writes long letters to the Germans, begging them to send home his father. But Carlotta usually takes his paper away and tears it up with the four little teeth that have just become visible, like grains of rice, against the pink velvet of her gums. . . ."

Good for you, Carlotta!

The Decline of Rosetta

October 15

In the latrines, a soldier is perching on the high wooden seat opposite mine. As he gets down, I can see a big tattooed picture on his left leg, just above the knee: a woman's profile and the name "Rosetta."

It seems as if his skin were so weary and slack that it had slipped down from his chest, where such pictures are usually to be found. I have a notion that when he pulls up his trousers, the loose skin will rise with them and return, bearing the tattooing with it, to its former position.

But when he does pull his trousers up, the skin fails to move, and Rosetta is left in her state of decline.

A Fistful of Earth

October 27

I pick up a fistful of earth and watch it run through my fingers, imagining a very ancient city. The history of a millennium has soaked into these walls; for nine hundred years this courtyard has been filled with shadows and for eight centuries the ground under that fortress has not seen the light of day. In the old building over there a prince was stabbed to death in 1472; here we have the thieves' quarter, which was depopulated by the plague of 1658. Children's bones lie deep in the sewers; walled up in thick pillars are the chained bodies of women buried alive. A thousand years of misery and happiness, shouts of sorrow and delight, words of love and hate have entered into these stones; the air is filled with crime, torture and lost lives. Every brick has absorbed a portion of men's existence; men's greasiness has polished the edges and corners, their breath has collected under vaults and ceilings, and every object is redolent of their bodily dissolution. The agglomeration of buildings has something human (like the wrapping of a mummy), and at the same time inhuman, about it. Something that has killed nature, something midway between an inanimate object and man.

The earth, too, seems to be overpowered and dead. Surely it is impossible that it should ever flower again or that among these age-old shadows the sun should ever shine. But suddenly a cataclysm reduces all the buildings to rubble, and men cart the rubble away. Here, now, is a field of waving grain. Here, where there is a clump of red poppies, there was once the dark hall of a house of ill fame, where unsmiling girls sat waiting. There, where the ears of wheat are heavy and golden, were torture chambers in which prisoners died of sheer terror.

This earth has canceled a millennium of history. Now it seems impossible that here the sun should ever have failed to shine. You pick a flower that has budded in a spot which used to be a harlot's chamber and ask your innocent child to take it to your mother.

Earth, like death, purifies everything. Earth, which is the end of all, is the eternal source of life. In this fistful of earth slipping between my fingers, there is a portion of past and a portion of future. I am the present, and I trample both future and past with my feet.

The Pendulum

The pendulum is an example of perpetual oscillation, disguised as an officer waiting to be sent home. At eight o'clock in the morning, the very instant that ranks are broken after roll call, he streaks like lightning toward his hut.

"Where are you going?"

"I'm going to pack my bags. The end of the war can't be more than a few hours away."

He disappears. But an hour later he is to be seen wandering alone about the camp, with a ravaged face, arms swinging at his sides and hands nearly touching his ankles, hair sticking to his forehead and his ears hanging as low as those of a setter.

"What's the matter?"

"I'll never have the strength to get through another winter. Another winter! Just think of that!"

With a deep sigh, he walks on, but no later than nine o'clock he bursts into the hut, bubbling over with joy.

"I'll exchange any amount of tobacco for a suitcase!

If anyone can let me have a bag, I'll leave him a big tin box of biscuits and my safety razor. I'm off, in a matter of minutes."

Twenty minutes later he's crouching near the rubbish hole, sobbing loudly and kissing the picture of his wife and children, his identification card and his commuter's railway ticket.

"When shall I see them again?" he moans, tearing his hair. "Perhaps never. Who knows when this war's going to be over? Nineteen forty-five, 1946, maybe 1948, for all I know."

At ten he comes back into the hut, through the window, positively oozing exhilaration.

"Have the departure orders come through?" he shouts. "Do we carry our heavy luggage, or are they sending a truck?"

With watch in hand, he swears that the end of the war is now a matter of seconds, and he is timing it. But two, five, ten minutes go by, and still the war is not over. The walking pendulum collapses into his bunk. Soon after this, he is seen with egg-size tears rolling down his cheeks, penning a letter.

"What are you doing now?"

"Writing my will. This war is going to last another twenty-five years, and I shan't survive it."

And so it goes, until late in the evening, when he finally decides to go to bed. But at midnight he wakes up with a start. "My wife!" he exclaims. "My children! Here I am! Come to my arms! It's over at last, and I've come home. You don't know how happy I am!"

When the reveille sounds the next morning, he lies supine in his bunk.

"Shake a leg!" we tell him. "Time to get up, and hurry!"

"I can't," he mutters in a faraway voice. "I was worn out and totally discouraged by waiting so many years for the war to come to an end. Put me down as having died in prison. And may my soul rest in peace!"

The Hesitator

A perpetual dilemma in the garb of an internee, this is the hesitator. He lives in a state of continuous tension, like a sprinter waiting for the hundred-yard race, or like a hunting dog, with tail erect, ears stiff and nose sniffing the air. As soon as he hears that the Commission for Repatriations is about to convene, he seeks out his companions.

"What are you going to do? What is he going to do? What are we going to do? What are they going to do?"

He dashes from right to left, into all the huts, up on every tier of bunks, through the washrooms, the infirmary, the latrines. He lays siege to the chaplain and begs him on bended knee to reveal God's will.

Having collected all the current opinions, he counts them up, weighs and divides them into "ayes" and "nays" and "maybes" and then lies flat on his bunk with his head between his hands and anxiously asks himself:

"What am *I* going to do?"

After a prolonged and painful delay he suddenly rushes to the hut where applications are being taken. On the tip of his tongue is:

"Yes!"

But in front of the door, doubt overtakes him and he says:

"No!"

Once he is back in his bunk, he has another brainstorm. Of course, the answer should have been:

"Yes."

He is off again, and this time he walks decisively into the seat of the Commission, signs the application with a firm hand and goes back to his own hut. But halfway there, he freezes into a dead stop.

"What if? . . ."

There's not a second to lose! He must change it at once. The slightest postponement might have fatal consequences. There he is, panting and harassed, before the Commission table. He signed up without thinking, he tells them. His best friend hasn't asked to go, and there is no question of separation. Finally he succeeds in recovering the application.

Soon he is once more in his own hut, about to lie down.

"Thank heaven, I put everything straight! I shouldn't want to live through minutes like those again!" But half-

way up to his bunk, a certain complication comes to
mind.

"What about? . . ."

Good God! Why hadn't he thought of that before?
What has he done? Dripping with cold sweat, hardly
seeing out of his eyes, he manages to run back to the
Commission. He has suffered an acute crisis, he explains,
elbowing his way forward, but now it is over. He pulls
out old Party membership cards, letters from his wife,
pictures of his children. Once more he makes formal application to be sent home. Then back, triumphantly, to
his own quarters. But at the sight of the door, he is
frozen again into immobility.

"The fact remains . . ."

*   *   *

Darkness has fallen and, in the middle of the empty
campground, a solitary figure crouches with his chin
resting on his knees and his hands running through his
hair.

"What's the matter?" asks a passerby.

A tragedy! In two seconds the Commission is going to
adjourn, and he is stuck midway between one hut and
the other, because he can't remember whether he was on
his way to re-sign the application or to re-withdraw it.

A Literary Poll

November 11

Extracts from the "want ads" tacked up on the latrine door.

Wanted to read, Florise, *a novel by Pignatelli. Will lend other novel, in exchange. Lieutenant Beccatelli, Hut 33-B.*

Will lend scientific volume, Sex and Love, *by Prof. De Napoli, in exchange for textbook of electro-technology or English grammar. Captain C. Luccioli, Hut 29-A.*

Will exchange Divine Comedy *for novel. Captain T.*

Exchange for cigarettes or tobacco:
  a) *Textbook of Calculus and Analytical Geometry (in French)*
  b) *Vitamin C capsules. Captain Birardi, Hut 29-A.*

Exchange Dante for textbook on photography. Lieutenant Terzolo, Hut 27-A.

Exchange History of Italian Literature in three volumes, by Vittorio Rossi, for tobacco or cigarettes. Lieutenant Rosario Lo Cascio. Hut 23-A.

Exchange Colerus' masterpiece, Mathematics Made Easy, *for German grammar. Lieutenant Rocco Mazzei, Hut 25-B.*

Free at Last

November 29

Somebody was a prisoner within me. He was shut up as if in a diving bell, and my fleshly garments and habits oppressed him. He looked out of my eyes, and his sight was keen, but my eyes were clouded over with the thick steam of conventional living.

His heart was shut up in mine and had to synchronize its beat with my sluggish pulsation. His voice was soft and clear, but my harsh voice would not let it be heard. Someone was a prisoner within me, and my thick hide bore down upon him, but now he has freed himself and gone away.

One day, as I trudged wearily over these deserted wastes, dragging my bones, heavy with nostalgia, behind me, I suddenly felt light as a feather and the sky seemed extraordinarily deep and blue. It was as if I had been looking at the world through a dirty window, and now the window had been thrown open. I saw a whole new world of the tiny details of things I had never seen before, and these details all fitted together to form a perfect whole. My ears, too, seemed to be unstopped, so that I could hear the slightest rustle. I heard unknown words and voices, which I thought belonged to inanimate things, but all along I was hearing my own voice, or rather that of my prisoner.

I turned around and saw that I had stepped out of myself and cast off my fleshly garment. I was free. My other self walked away and with him all my earthly affections, leaving only their essence behind. As if a flower had been taken away from me, leaving its perfume in my nostrils and its color in my eyes.

Shall I encounter my other self again? Will he be waiting, outside the enclosure, to repossess me? Shall I go home weighed down by my old, fleshly shell?

If so, dear God, let my imprisonment never come to an end. Don't take my freedom away.

Carlotta

I'll never forget the night of December 30, 1943. It was around two o'clock, as I remember, and the agitation of the wind roused me from my slumbers.

"Tomorrow morning," I thought to myself, "all those strips of tarred paper that the wind has torn off the roof will be stuck in the barbed-wire fence or scattered over the sand, like shreds of night."

Then, satisfied with my observation, I prepared to go back to sleep. But all of a sudden a man in a nightshirt appeared beside my bunk and said in a low voice, pointing me out to someone he had brought with him:

"He's that fellow there."

At once I recognized the little man who had come to visit me at Czestochowa on the night of October 27 and called the German eagle a chicken. But this time it was a much more serious matter than before. At the age of only three and a half years, the wretched boy was no longer content merely to haunt adult dreams; he had now taken up with dubious company as well.

I was reminded of *La Traviata,* the beloved Alfredo and the proud words of the noble de Germont. For the sight that met my eyes was one to make a father blush. A woman stood at my son's side, and obviously she was no better than she should be since she was wearing a night-shirt and a cap, all askew, on her head, while a lock of hair hung down over her left eye. What's more, she was unsteady on her pins and had to cling to her companion in crime. And all the time she was chewing gum, like a low-grade taxi girl in a dive in South Philadelphia.

"There he is," said the young man. "Go ahead and touch him. He won't bite."

The miserable female displayed no emotion. Why should one of her kind take any interest in a family man who retained his full dignity, even although he laid his head on a foreign pillow?

"Who is she?" I asked severely, with my head emerging from under the blanket.

"Just a friend," Albertino answered calmly.

When my father came to visit me, two years after I had left my native heath, he found me eating my dinner in the company of a young woman he had never seen before. He asked me who she was and I replied, quite simply:

"My wife."

My father nodded his head in approval and did not

question me further. I was thirty years old, and we had long since agreed that each of us was to live his own life. Thirty-two years before, my father had got married without asking my permission, so it was logical enough that I should do the same thing.

Now, however, in view of Albertino's tender age, I had a right, as a father, to demand that he give me further information about his female companion. I did demand it, and in reply he told me a truly pitiful tale.

The girl had come, one rainy night, to Albertino's house. And her misfortunes were such that she couldn't be turned away, especially on account of a big green-eyed cat, which would have eaten her up and then serenely licked its chops. Yes, that is the story, just as Albertino told it to me with a graphic demonstration of how the anthropophagous cat would have licked its whiskers after the succulent meal. He added that among the poor girl's misfortunes was the fact that she had never known her father, a bad man who had come to a bad end in prison. It was in order to show her what a father was like that he had brought her to see me, a good man, who couldn't possibly come to a bad end.

"My father's good," he told her. "He's a miwitawy internee."

"Everyone ought to be good," I said severely. And I suggested that since the girl's father was so nefarious an individual, perhaps I could temporarily take his place. After all, I had plenty of time to spare.

"This father is mine," Albertino was saying, with corrugated brow. And he put his finger on my forehead in order to show exactly which father he was talking about and preclude any misunderstanding.

I looked at the girl and shook my head. Poor thing, she couldn't have been more than forty days old, and to see her wandering about the icy dreams of a Polish night was extremely distressing. And then her features were somehow familiar to me. What was that resemblance? Somewhere I had seen those eyes before, and also the dimple in the middle of that chin. I told Albertino to take her home and put her to bed.

"But where's she to sleep?" I asked him.

"In papa's place, in the big bed."

This was a serious case of usurpation, but it served, indirectly, to mitigate the bleakness of the miserable bed assigned to me by the law.

"Only she does messy things," Albertino added.

"What messy things?"

For an answer he pointed to the puddle of water on the floor. But just then we were interrupted by the approach of heavy footsteps from the other end of the hut.

"It's the man with the gun in front of the garden gate," whispered Albertino in alarm. "Make him go away, Papa."

"I can't do that yet," I answered. "You'd better be the one to go."

And he went off, dragging the little girl behind him like a rag doll.

No, I'll never forget the night of December 30, 1943, or the morning of December 31, either. When I woke up I thought right away of the strange story of the past night. The wall of the hut had swallowed up the two sleepwalkers. The last thing I had seen was a round eye, and eventually this had darkened in color and melted into a knot in the wood. There was the knot, round as an *O,* and there, on the floor below my bunk, was a trace of the wet spot, described by Albertino as "messy," a sample of the messes now to be found on my side of the big bed, at home.

And I remember the evening of that same December 31, when I received my first postcard, whose message began with the seven wonderful words: "On November 13 was born Signorina Carlotta."

*   *   *

Oh, Signorina Carlotta, born on the first line of a free postcard, like a pink flower growing out of the snow, or rather a flower that blossomed late, in the Indian summer of that southern clime, and here only on the chilly last day of the year! Forty-eight days I had to wait, thanks to the postal bureaucracy, but you made the time shorter by one day.

For you were the visitor of the night of December 30, at whom I looked askance because you were chewing gum, you were unsteady on your pins and you had a right eye as round as that of your father.

Signorina Carlotta, I know where the unfortunate woman who made me a parent found that exotic name of yours, with its revolutionary flavor. Carlotta is what I called the wild and woolly heroine of my latest novel, which for some reason particularly appealed to your mother. Do you see what may be the results of mis-

guided reading? What if I had dubbed my heroine Cri-
milde or Zebedea? What would have happened to you
then?

I'll never forget the night of December 30, 1943.
Among the hundred thousand names registered in the
postoffice of an internment camp, a new name, Carlotta,
was about to take its place. Clothed in the beam of a
searchlight playing upon the window of my hut, this
name made itself known to me, before I ever saw it in
writing. And with it came that other name, Albertino,
not so very much older.

"Let's go," he said to you, "and I'll show you my
father. "There's the place where he's sleeping."

The agitation of the wind on the roof of Hut No. 18
awakened me. I saw my son again and made the acquaintance of my daughter. Now, as the days drag on, I
am waiting for her to return.

More News from Abroad

December 19

A letter from home:

"Carlottina has four teeth, and she has learned to say:
'No.'"

I've learned to say "No" too. But it took a world war
to teach me.

Solitude

December 31

The stuffing of my mattress has turned to dust and in it my bones are swimming about. I feel like a man drifting, shipwrecked, on the open sea.

The Seasons

Once upon a time there were seasons, which changed punctually, every three months, in accordance with the design of the Celestial Powers. And every season had its fruits. Spring brought new grass, sweet-smelling milk and butter; summer, blond wheat and crusty, white bread; autumn, golden grapes and sparkling wine; winter, savory chestnuts.

But those were the happy times when the year began on the first of January. Then they switched its beginning, and the whole pattern of the seasons was broken. The only fruit any of them bore was turnips.

The Tablecloth

Once upon a time there was such a thing as a tablecloth, a white rectangle of civilization. On it there gleamed glass, china and silver, and around it there gathered, twice a day, a mother's gaily flowered dresses, children's rosy cheeks and golden hair, and the black, handlebar mustache and blessed appetite of a father.

In the middle there was a carafe of red Chiaretto wine and, all around, like cotton-stuffed birds, hovered strains of radio music. Also in the air were the fragrant odors of soup and bread, golden particles of sunshine that came through the window, the reflections of the youngest child's aluminum highchair and the transparent dreams of a china cat, which lay curled up on the sideboard, near a red vase filled with bright yellow flowers.

Once upon a time there was a tablecloth, the immaculately white meeting place of a family's hands. On it there glided to rest, like dead leaves, wearied by their brief flight, the important words spoken in the course of the daylight hours.

Afterward, the crumbs and the weary words were brushed away. The rectangle folded up its whiteness like the uncut pages of a book, and went to gossip, with the fragrant drawer of the sideboard, about the scandalous doings of the day.

"In the soup there was a grain of rice still clothed in its husk!"

"Incredible!" commented the drawer.

Once upon a time there was a tablecloth, and a grain of rice with a husk on had something scandalous about it. But those were the times when, although you couldn't call a spade a spade, nevertheless soup was still soup.

The Colonel

Once upon a time there was a colonel, with an important white mustache and a sword at his side, who had a way of making surprise visits to the barracks. Only there was always a bugle to report his arrival.

Then things happened the way they do in a moving-picture film when the projector comes to a stop. In the smithy the blacksmiths stood with upraised hammers; in the gymnasium the acrobats paused in mid-air; in the stable the trotting horses froze into bronze, with three hoofs suspended and one touching the ground; in the kitchen the boiling pots were still; at the tailor's, the drop which was falling from the tailor's nose hung on an invisible thread six inches above the floor; in the hall the clock stopped ticking and the pendulum was left on the upward stroke; in the infirmary the microbes inside the patients interrupted their maleficent activity.

But at the second blast of the bugle, everything returned to life.

When the colonel said to a soldier: "Well done!" the soldier did not dare wash his ear for fear of interfering with the vibrations which these words had communicated to his tympanum. All his life long, he would hear the echo of the colonel's words of praise.

But those were the times when rivers murmured placidly as they ran their course to the sea. After that, murmuring was forbidden, and the rivers said no more, even when whole trainloads of colonels crossed the railroad bridges.

1945

1 9 4 5

The Resurrection of Words

January 5, 1945

He is quite aware of the fact that he is repeating himself, and yet he does not search for new words. Here
everything is repeated; every day and every dream is just
like the one that went before, and his vocabulary obeys
the same law. But every word swells into a whole chap-
ter: country, freedom, morals, conscious, love, honesty.
Words become concepts.

Tales of Wietzendorf

January 7

The "labor captain" called a meeting, in the hut used
as a theatre, of sixty "technicians," chosen at random,

and spoke of the opportunities of collaborating with the Germans in the effort to save Europe from Bolshevism. He spoke of the inevitable victory of the German *Reich* and hinted at the existence of decisive new weapons; then, in conclusion, he declared himself ready to take the names of volunteers. Although only sixty so-called technicians had been invited, those present numbered five hundred and, in order to make himself perfectly clear, he added:

"We need men who really want to work for us. All those that don't feel they can put their heart in their work may as well leave right now."

With which, every last man went out of the room, and the captain, left alone with the interpreter, could only mumble: "The lazy dogs!" and put his fountain pen back in his pocket.

The Search

January 15

Bewildered young men are searching, with great good will, for the truth.

"We need someone to teach us, to start us out on the right way. We've plenty of time, and among us there are some very good scholars. We ought to have courses."

This germ of teachability is in their blood. Courses, that's all they want, courses in reconstruction, in the life of tomorrow, in politics and the practice of liberty.

But truth can't be taught; every man has to discover and master it as an individual; he must think for himself and create a conscience of his own. It's no use searching for someone else who will think for you and teach you how to be free. Here are the effects, now trace the cause and single out the mistake. You must separate yourself from the masses and the masses' collective thinking, like a pebble from a gravel walk, recover an individual personality and conscience, in short, raise a moral issue.

Tomorrow, as soon as your feet touch your native soil, you'll find half a dozen men, each one anxious to teach you the truth, in terms that differ widely among them. While you're still here, you must prepare, make yourselves free, so as not to become a prisoner of the first man that accosts you as you come out of the station. You must sift every word you hear in your own conscience, and see through each one's falsities to the truth.

We, the Poor

January 20

A small crowd has gathered around the Capuchin Father, who is our chaplain, to hear him talk about the soup he and his fellow monks used to distribute to the poor. At the request of those present, he gives the exact measures of every ingredient:

"Cabbage, three-eighths of a pound; horse fat, one ounce . . ."

How low we have sunk, that we should find enjoyment in the description of a breadline!

Notes

January 21

When you're loosening a board from one of the huts for your own personal use, or doing something else contrary to regulations, there's always a practical joker who comes up behind you and shouts something in German to make you jump a mile.

*   *   *

"What have you brought me?" my son will ask me when I come home.

"A brand new father," would be the wisecracking reply. But I shan't make it. This "new man" pose is as old as the hills, along with the rest.

*   *   *

International conventions regarding prisoners and internees should contain a clause to the effect that they

are never to be without tobacco. This is an obvious way
to curtail the brutality of war.

* * *

Every now and then someone dies within us. We die,
little by little every day, until finally the last of our
selves is dead.

* * *

I don't really believe half of what I say.

More Tales of Wietzendorf

January 23

Lieutenant X. was impelled by hunger to catch, kill and
cook a puppy which he found wandering incautiously
about the camp. The fact was discovered, and the lieutenant was placed under arrest for "eating a small dog
belonging to the German command."

While he was in confinement he grew so melancholy
that he would wake up in the middle of a bad dream,
shouting that the dog had attacked him. In order to
calm him down, someone had to pretend to take a shotgun and shoot the assailant.

"Bang! Bang! Dead as a doornail!"

Soon he had to be taken to a sanatorium at Hamburg
and, when he returned two months later, the Germans
said he was cured. He was indeed very quiet, and the

dog no longer seemed to be on his mind. But after he had been back a few hours he got up on the big brick oven and insisted on eating his food and relieving himself there. And he wouldn't get down until they came and took him away to the sanatorium again.

Hope

January 25

Captain P. died of malnutrition in the infirmary. Eighteen months ago, a few days before he was captured by the Germans in France, he had bought three bars of chocolate to take to his children.

The three chocolate bars followed him into deportation and hunger. He kept them all the time in the shreds of his mattress, taking them out to look at once in a while and thinking of his children's joy.

He died of malnutrition in the infirmary, clutching the chocolate bars in his hand.

Nothing ever Happens

January 29

Nothing ever happens, and yet something has got to

happen soon. The calendar is filled with black crosses, with days wiped out forever. Obviously time has been passing by.

Hunger

January 31

For eighteen months now I've suffered from hunger, and yet every day the sensation seems new.

The Rag Man

The rag man isn't the supporter of a political party that stands for reducing the world to rags and tatters, although that would seem to benefit his trade, and such a party has existed since the world began. No, he is a strict individualist, and any stand he may take is purely his own.

Originally, the rag man looked just like the next fellow. Most likely he wore one of those suburban length jackets that came down below the knee, with pockets as large as parcel post mailboxes, and carried a briefcase so smartly styled that it was called an attaché case instead, and after he entered the cavalry his triple-spurred boots had a gadget that clicked whenever he snapped to attention.

But as soon as he reached the internment camp, the rag man's esthetic values suffered an overnight change. It was as if he had been first dipped in glue and then rolled through a pile of rubbish. He appeared in a garment studded from head to foot with red, green, blue, black and yellow patches, with tin can tops, metal buttons, ends of wire, rope and ribbon, wood chips, leather findings, fragments of cardboard and plastic. Rigged up in this style, the fellow was no longer a man; he was the embodiment of a five year plan for economic self-sufficiency, a walking thrift shop, an international salvaging company, a world's fair of synthetics.

But the rag man was not yet happy; an ambitious dream still haunted his brain. He wanted to go home with a patch of green wool over the left buttock, in place of the three square inches of skin traded for cigarettes, with a piece of wood supporting his leg where the tibia used to be and a box of sand occupying the space left empty when he bartered his brain for a tin of sweet tobacco.

The "Whose-is-This" Man

The distributing officer or "rationeer," relying on a pair of scales, his own previous experience and the brotherly advice of all his fellow officers around the table, has di-

vided into twenty-two parts the potatoes, brought in a
great aluminum pail by the officer of the day.

Next on the job is the "equalization committee,"
headed by the room leader. After an animated discussion, shared by all those present, this committee proceeds to transfer the potatoes to the plates, in such a way
that all the portions shall be equal not only in quantity
but in quality as well.

But these proceedings must now be submitted to pop-
ular approval. Lieutenant A. states that the first portion
is twice as large as the second, while Captain B. insists
that, on the contrary, the second is three times larger
than the first. When it seems that there is no hope of a
compromise solution, then there has to be a re-check all
the way through.

A dozen or so weighings are effected on two different
pairs of scales, with the hut leader called in as supreme
witness and arbiter. Justice triumphs, agreement is complete, and general satisfaction is expressed in the unani-
mous vote:

"Good! Let's eat!"

At this point we have the appearance of the "whose-
is-this" man.

*   *   *

This important character, a gentleman above reproach, penetratingly passes in review his twenty-one
fellow officers, who stand motionless and silent before
him, like the figures in a frieze of Corporate Justice.
Finally he looks one of them straight in the eye and calls
out:

"Captain Cognacchi!"

Captain Cognacchi steps forward and goes to stand in the farthest corner of the room, his face to the wall and his back to the assembly. Then the whose-is-this man points at random to one of the plates on the table.

"Whose is this?" he asks severely.

"Lieutenant Bruscoli's," answers Captain Cognacchi, taking care not to budge an inch from the wall.

And so it goes on, for twenty more questions and answers. After the final distribution is over, every one of the twenty-two internees goes back to his own place and starts to peel his potatoes, not without muttering:

"I've been cheated again!"

*   *   *

In the tragic September of 1943, when we found ourselves suddenly transported to a *Lager,* far from our homes and families, and uncertain as to what was going to happen to them, one particular problem tormented the sanest among us.

"What measures shall we take to assure absolute justice?"

Even with the help of scales, calipers, measuring cups, spoons and slide rulers, it turned out to be almost impossible to divide a cube of margarine, a paralleliped of bread or a pail of potatoes into equal parts. We could figure it out to the nearest ounce, but not to the nearest grain, and Justice is essentially a matter of grains. And it seemed inevitable that the fellow assigned to do the distributing should favor his best friends. For a while, we tried leaving it to chance: to playing cards, improvised roulette wheels, to a jar full of numbered balls and, finally, to the same jar plus a separate safety cover.

This last system was particularly ingenious. After the rations had been divided, the plates were lined up on the table and covered with a piece of canvas. The officer assigned to the jar, or "extractor," drew out a ball and, without looking at it, held it in his fist, which he raised into the air, shouting: "Ready!" At the same time, another man, designated as "pointer," who had been previously blindfolded, stuck one hand under the canvas and drew out the first plate which it touched. Then the extractor opened his hand and showed the number which he had drawn. "Eighteen!" The officer designated by this number took the plate away, never failing to mumble, as a matter of course:

"I've been cheated again!"

But most of the systems excogitated in this way had a fatal flaw of some kind. When finally an anonymous benefactor invented the "whose-is-this?" method, we breathed a sigh of relief and our confinement began to weigh less heavily upon us.

*   *   *

"Whose is this?"

For months our daily existence has been keynoted by this cry. Every time an object of any kind enters the hut there is a whose-is-this man ready to step into the role of Great Adjudicator. Only one thing, so far, has eluded his grasp. But it wouldn't in the least surprise me, if tomorrow he laid hands on the mail sack and shouted:

"Whose is this letter? Whose is this postcard?"

One day he too will return to his home and family. He'll take up the burden of everyday life, but it will be an endless series of interrogations:

"Whose is this train? Whose is this taxi? Whose is this elevator? Whose is this wife? Whose is this salary? Whose is this automobile trip? Whose is this stroke of apoplexy that has just laid me low? Whose is this funeral procession? Whose is this Last Judgment? Whose is this Heaven?"

"Mine! Mine! Mine!"

Amen.

Business

February 15

The sentries shoot into the air but the business deals with the French officers go right on. We Italians throw our bread rations over the fence and they toss back packages of cigarettes. Today a French captain protested loudly:

"That's not honest! That's not fair!"

And, to be sure, it wasn't. An Italian got the Frenchman's cigarettes in advance, and then tossed back a bag full of sand.

No, it was not honest, Monsieur. But is it honest or fair for a neatly and warmly dressed Frenchman, nourished on the contents of parcels sent him by Pétain's

France and the International Red Cross, to trade five of the Camels which the United States sends, three hundred per month per man, to every internee of potential military interest, for the bread ration of a poor devil of an Italian who has been hungry for eighteen months on end and seeks only a moment's release from hunger and homesickness in a few puffs of tobacco?

No, Monsieur; that's not honest, that's not fair.

Chip

I knew an internee so small that he could sleep in a mess bowl; he could even stretch out to his full length and still have room left over, because he was only six inches high.

At that time I was in a camp somewhere in Poland. The reason we knew it was Poland was that the bread was round, whereas in Germany it had been rectangular. Yes, we were properly grateful to Divine Providence for this variation in the shape of the bread, because we had no other means of telling where we were. Every *Lager* is just like the next: a giant sandbox with a lid of melancholy.

The days passed dully and equally by. It seemed as if nothing could ever happen and we were forgotten by God and man. But one February morning there was something new, and we realized that death had remembered. I found myself the possessor of a photograph, hanging somewhere between my head and neck, a photograph that had lost its father.

I had come across the photograph on the ground three evenings before and on the back there was penciled a name I had never heard. I asked around and was directed to one of the huts, but there I heard that the owner had been sent to the infirmary. All I could do was wait for him to come out, and I didn't dream that he would never come.

The photograph was postcard size, and the subject was a curly-haired, smiling little boy two years old, sitting bolt upright in a baby carriage. I adopted the fatherless thing and nailed it over my bunk. Every time I went to sleep or woke up, it seemed to me that the little boy was smiling.

But one morning there was no smile. I scanned the photograph thoroughly, holding it up to the light and under a magnifying glass, but the baby was gone. The carriage was still there, but it was empty. I reached out for the heap of ragged clothing at the foot of my bunk and involuntarily shuddered. Something warm and squirming had touched my hand. A little boy six inches high was sleeping in a fold of my wool-lined jacket. And he was the one that had been in the photograph before.

I took some of the wool lining out of the jacket, laid it in the bottom of my mess bowl and put the baby to rest there. He went right on sleeping, breathing as lightly as the shadow of a flower, and I gazed at him out of one, half-closed eye because I was afraid that the weight of my total gaze might be too much for his frail little body.

Six-inch-long little boy, already as much of a prisoner as if you were a grown man, why did you get out of your baby carriage, why did you abandon your happy world of shiny photographic paper? What can you want with our ice-cold melancholy? Beyond the barbed-wire enclosure, under the gnarled trees of the low-lying hill which cuts off our view, black crosses stud the potter's field, the dead men's dormitory. A little to the right side, on a slope midway between the hill and the enclosure, there is a smaller field, bounded by a white wooden fence, apparently set out for our special benefit. For whereas living prisoners are all on the same level, and a Mongol shepherd is treated just like a Latin intellectual, dead ones are apparently subject to differentiation. Otherwise, when Civilization comes to draw up its final balance sheet, the job of counting the recently sprouted crosses might be a source of confusion.

"What an unholy mess!"

For Civilization wants men to be divided, even in death, into the categories of Russian, German, English, Italian, French, all enemies after death, just as they were when they were alive. And yet there are no frontiers in Death's kingdom.

During the still nights, when there is a lull in the wind which sweeps by day over the vast Polish plain, thousands upon thousands of men wander among the gnarled trees on the hillside; their bodies mingle one with the other and pass through the wooden crosses, because they are creatures not of substance but of memory.

In the small field bounded by the white fence there is so far only one cross, with a name and number upon it. From the larger cemetery ghosts wander down to lean against the fence. In spent, echo-like voices they call out:

"Italianski! Italianski!"

And when a single ghost emerges from below the single cross and comes to answer, they add:

"Italianski! Brot!"

They offer him bread and salt, but he throws out his arms in refusal because he has nothing to give them in return, having been taken prisoner empty-handed. The visitors shake their heads and smile. They want nothing, need nothing.

Suddenly someone comes from even farther away, someone whom they all know. Until not very long ago, he was a sentry on the watchtower, with a revolver on his belt and a machine gun within easy reach; at night he played a searchlight over the camp, causing the frost on the barbed wire to glimmer. Woe to anyone that came too near! He would have pitilessly shot down a prisoner who went even half an inch beyond the warning wire, which set off the zone where no trespassing was permitted. Now the other ghosts recognize him, but none of them worries about being caught out of bounds. One morning he fell, stiff with cold, from the watchtower and they carried him to the infirmary. Now here he is, a shade among shades. He was buried in the village cemetery, but every evening he comes for a chat in this place. They speak different languages but, even so, they understand each other perfectly, and they talk of good, innocent things.

"My house is on the edge of the steppe, as if it were on the bank of a body of green water," a bearded *moujik* was saying.

"I used to go every Sunday on the ferris wheel in the Prater," said the sentry. "From up there, I could look out over all of Vienna."

And the Italian ghost put in:

"My little boy's two years old, and I only wish I could show you his last picture. But it slipped out of my pocket when they were carrying me to the infirmary. Too bad, because it was such a good likeness! If you could have seen him sitting, with a broad smile on his face, in his carriage! . . ."

*　　　　*　　　　*

The little boy lay asleep in my mess bowl and I looked at him, shaking my head.

"What do you want with our ice-cold melancholy?" I asked him. "Your eyes can't see the ghosts that people the empty nights of the *Lager*. Go back to your happy world of shiny photographic paper!"

But he stayed with me, as the private ghost of my "castle." I lived, at this time, in a castle minus towers. Two bunks, one on top of the other, with four wooden posts to support them. I lived on the ground floor, and the other fellow above me. In order to protect myself from draughts I had suspended old mattress covers from one post to another. Other people couldn't see in, but I could see out, dimly, and everything in the room seemed to move as if in a dream.

There was a danger that during my absence the little boy might slip down from behind this curtain and fall onto the floor, and I didn't want anyone else to see him. A man who has been palming himself off as a bachelor can't suddenly be found with a baby in his bunk! People are so malicious, there was no telling what they would say.

So I took a wooden board and drove nails in all around the outer edge, connecting them with several rounds of string, in such a way as to make a miniature internment camp. Poor little six-inch fellow, he had just as much of a right as we to be a prisoner, since he too had done no one any harm!

I hung the board from the headpiece of the bunk and made a small hole in my improvised curtain, at the end nearest the window, so that the little boy might have his ration of sun. I gave him a name as small as he, a name made from that of his father. His father was called Cipriano and the boy, from this day on, Chip.

Chip spent his days shut up in the miniature *Lager*. He played with a gilt button from my blue sweater and I never failed to give him his ration of food: one gram of margarine, two of jam, three of bread and five of green peas.

One day he pointed to my identification tag, obviously wanting to have one like it. Why not? I made him

a miniature copy, and engraved on it the number *oo1*.
He wanted a pair of wooden shoes, too, like mine, and
I carved them out of a piece of soft wood. After that,
whenever he walked, the board floor of his camp made
a creaking sound, as if there were a worm inside. Every
now and then I sent him a parcel containing a quarter
of a piece of hard candy, a square of chocolate, three
drops of condensed milk, etc., in fact samples of almost
everything you can think of with the exception of medicines, inflammable objects and tools which could be
used to effect an escape.

" 'oon," he said one evening, pointing to the "castle"
roof. He wanted his share of moon, and I gave it to him.
I rigged up a tiny, round mirror and opened a hole in
the curtain so that a ray of electric light could beat upon
it. And by means of some cotton wool I provided him
with his share of clouds.

"Sea," he would say every now and then. At such
times I hid him in my coat pocket and we went out together. In one corner of the camp there was a small
pond. I made him captain of one of my wooden shoes.
He sailed blissfully from one shore to the other and
even made a landing in force, the prelude to a full-scale
invasion, several times over.

Twice a day I sounded the bugle by blowing on the
edge of a piece of tissue paper. At once Chip ran to the
center of his *Lager* and stood at attention, just as he had
seen the rest of us stand, while I passed him in review.
There was never a single absence on his record.

But one day at the end of March, Chip did not answer

the roll call. We had packed our bags in preparation for being moved to another *Lager,* and I was worried about the possibility of a final inspection. Where was I to hide Chip? And what if they found him? Would they take him away, or would they simply stamp him with their *Geprüft* mark? I might get into real hot water. And in an hour we were to be all ready to go. I decided to slip him under my cap, with instructions to hold on tight to my hair. But when I started to take him out of my bunk, I found his *Lager* empty. The string of the fence had been cut and Chip had run away. I looked in my knapsack, my mattress and everywhere else I could think of, but Chip was nowhere to be found. I couldn't even find the photograph, which on the morning of this same day had been hanging at the head of my bed.

Gusts of wind swept at intervals through that dreary March day. Every now and then a window swung open and scraps of paper and clothing, thrown onto the floor of the hut, flew up into the air. The improvised curtain had come loose, on the side nearer the window, and perhaps the photograph had been blown away. But not so Chip. Chip had made his escape.

I wandered through the deserted camp, calling him by name. Eventually I came to the place, at one end, which afforded a view of the field bounded by a white wooden fence and its one solitary grave. On the tombstone there, something like a piece of cardboard, was the photograph of a little boy, smiling from his baby carriage. Chip had at last found the man he had come to seek in our ice-cold melancholy, and he had returned to his happy world of shiny photographic paper. I was going away, but Chip was staying with his father.

Once upon a time I knew an internee only so big. Name: Chip; identification tag number: *001;* name of camp: Far away.

The Day

And so it came about that on the afternoon of April 22, 1945, I found myself suddenly face to face with 1,200 pounds of sugar.

In order to see this event in its true perspective, we must remember that if we add the number of calories in our daily camp rations to the number we had tucked away in reserve under our skins, we should reasonably have been dead for 471 days. Apparently, if an Italian sets his mind on living, you simply can't kill him.

Well then, to make a long story short, 471 days after I should have died, I found myself the unexpected proprietor, pro tem, of Hermann Shoert's grocery store in the town of Bergen. It was April 22, 1945, and I remember distinctly how, after I had finished the sixth pound of sugar, I began to feel very, very hungry.

I have prefaced my story with this explanation in order that my readers may understand the exact state of mind of the group of internees to which I belonged, when they took over a pleasant little town, stocked with everything the heart could desire, whence all the inhabitants had fled.

Here They Come!

April 16

At half past five in the afternoon, everyone began shouting: "Here they come!" and rushing toward the gate. There were six thousand of us, counting both French and Italians, but I managed to climb up on one of the posts supporting the barbed-wire fence, and it was from this vantage point that I saw the liberators. They came in a medium-sized black car and all of them were engaging in appearance, especially Major Cooley, who had round, rosy cheeks like those of the jolly drinkers in the multi-colored liquor advertisements of the Christmas issue of *Esquire*. The other two were a Scottish corporal and a Canadian soldier, each armed with a machine gun.

The major disarmed the German guards at the gate and turned over both men and arms to the French. This was logical enough because, although they had been interned ever since the encirclement of the Maginot Line, these good fellows had taken the attitude that they were winning the war, alongside the Allies. Unlike the Russians and ourselves, they had received parcels from the International Red Cross. And because they had been for only a few days in this melancholy last camp, they had a martial air, enhanced by their stiff caps with the red top and the black cross on it, which always reminded me of the bottom side of our No. 149 grenade, practice type.

After this, all three liberators advanced into the camp, and an incident occurred which the Frenchmen found particularly puzzling. The Gestapo had made frequent inspections and searches, carried out with such meticulous care as to be positively indecent. Nevertheless, after nineteen months of internment, we were able to display cameras by the dozen and an Italian flag twelve by fifteen feet in size, whereas the Frenchmen could not come out with a single cockade. Italians are gifted this way. Once in Poland, when we were being transferred from one camp to another, I saw a Sicilian lieutenant emerge from the search hut clad in nothing but a shirt, which was the only garment they had left on him, and carrying the rest of his clothes in his arms with, hidden among them, a big six-tube radio.

I myself am the least scheming man in the world, and in January, 1945, when we were in the process of shifting from one camp to another and they took all our blankets away because they said the bombed-out inhabitants of Hamburg and Bremen needed them more badly than we, they deprived me of the scarf I had made myself out of a piece of heavy woolen cloth. I came out of the search shivering and groaning, but in my duffel bag I still had my old seven by eight barracks blanket. Now that I am home I have given it to little Albertino, and every time I look at it I say: "Hello, old thing, I haven't forgotten that you saved my life, you know."

Italians know very well how to "operate"; indeed, this negative quality has done them, as a nation, a great deal of harm. But while we were interned, it had its positive side, particularly in the spontaneous generation of radios. A single tube was all that was needed; everything else was made on the spot, including earphones and batteries. The final product could be set up in a mess bowl, and the system worked so fast that when Churchill spoke, for instance, the first part of his speech was being circulated in Italian before the rest was over.

When it's a question of "making a fool" of somebody, we Italians consider that our national prestige is involved, and do perfectly incredible things. For example, Signor M., a stoutish, dignified and aloof gentleman, once went over to the motor bike which a Gestapo sergeant left every day just outside the hut used as a post office. Right under the eyes of the sentry on the nearby tower, he detached the dynamo, carried it to a solitary spot, took it apart, unwound a long piece of copper wire and then returned it to where he had found it. In this way he secured the coil necessary for his radio.

Let's be quite frank: I may be an Italian, but I like my compatriots, in spite of it. Every man is entitled to a weakness of his own!

*   *   *

The liberators saluted the biggest flag they could see and then went away, assuring us that regular forces would arrive the next morning.

A few hours later somebody noticed that on the farthest watchtower a sentry was still standing, quite unim-
pressed, with gun in hand. No one had told him anything, and as far as he was concerned the war was still
going on, just as it was for a certain well-known super-
annuated Italian marshal. They shouted out what had
happened, and the old watchdog nodded his head to
show that he understood, then slowly came down from
the tower and walked over toward the guardhouse and
capitulation.

"Why don't you go on home?" someone yelled at him,
but he shook his head and continued on his fatal way.
Probably he didn't have too much confidence in his fellow Germans.

An International Mess

April 17

This morning we woke up to find a typed announce-
ment from the Italian command of the camp, to the
effect that our sufferings were now over and we were
free to go home and join the effort of reconstruction.
It wound up with three lines in capital letters: HUR-
RAH FOR ITALY! HURRAH FOR THE ALLIES!
. . . and another hurrah, I don't remember for what.

This disturbed me greatly. Our superiors had laid
their hands on paper, a typewriter and an official seal.

Who was to save us from Orders of the Day, and so on? The Good Lord had saved us from the Germans, but we had no right to expect the impossible of Him. A military command with paper, seal and typewriter is quite capable of eluding even divine control.

"We've got to watch out," I said to Arturo. "Before we know it, we'll have returned to inspections, reviews, guard duty, and yellow envelopes with arrest records."

"You mean they've found yellow envelopes, too?"

"It looks that way."

"Then we're done for," Arturo admitted gloomily.

But the Good Lord did continue to help us. In the afternoon, the major came back and told us that other troops were coming soon. Sure enough, a few minutes after his departure, a squad of soldiers armed with machine guns and submachine guns appeared upon the scene. Only, instead of being English, they were German.

So it was that we escaped from the threat of Orders of the Day. But the Germans gave at least one man a lot of trouble. And that man was a German.

When you tell the story this way, the war comes to seem one huge joke. But appearances are deceiving. Everything is relative and depends on the point of view. For instance, it wasn't much of a joke to poor "Captain Armistice," when they strung him up on a rope.

Captain Armistice

He came to the *Lager* of Sandbostel in the autumn of 1944; he was afflicted with asthma and it was plain to see that he put no stock in secret weapons or ultimate victory. For this reason he was dubbed "Captain Armistice," and if he hadn't had the unpardonable defect of being a German, he would certainly have been defined as a "good man."

This doesn't mean that in Germany there are no good people. Of course, all Germans are born bad, because that is regulations, and in their country regulations are sacred. But little by little, as they acquire the faculty of reason, they redeem themselves and become almost affable. These redeemed souls are easily distinguishable from the rest, because over them is a tablet with the plainly printed words: HIER RÜHT IN GOTT (Here rests in God).

Although Captain Armistice was a live German, he often managed to be as agreeable as a dead one. Probably because he felt himself so fatally close to the hour of redemption that he unconsciously put on the moral garb and positive qualities that usually belong only to the German dead, as they rest in the Everlasting Arms.

When we were transferred to Wietzendorf, Captain Armistice and his asthma came along. Then, on the morning of April 13, we were awakened by the joyous cry: "The Germans are gone!" Even when we poured out of the huts and saw the German sentries still on the watchtowers, our enthusiasm was not dampened. The half dozen remaining German soldiers were so old and infirm that they hardly added up, all together, to a single dead man and, to cap it all, Captain Armistice was their leader. And, as I have hinted before, he was not so much a captain with asthma as asthma with a captain. And asthma knows no nationality.

The allied troops had arrived at Hannover and were proceeding toward Celle. Under these circumstances, the enemy command had decided to abandon the camp by night, taking all able-bodied men along, and leaving the supervision of the three thousand French and three thousand Italian internees to Captain Armistice and the glorious relics of what had such a short time ago been the proudest army in the world.

All is Lost Except for the Regulations

On that same day of April 13, something very serious happened. The Italian command nailed up a paper entitled "Permanent Orders, Number One," composed of six paragraphs, one of which contained seven highly important prohibitions; the fifth was positively historical, stating, as it did, that: "the aforementioned soldiers are hereby obliged to observe the order and discipline proscribed by the regulations of the Royal Italian Army, failing which observance they are subject to the punishments set forth by both military and civilian law."

After this several internees nearly died—one actually did die—of intestinal occlusion because they had broken into the supplies of potatoes. A little later, German reenforcements arrived and installed their artillery all around the camp. They were prevented from setting up an anti-tank gun only twelve or fifteen feet from the barbed-wire fence by Colonel Duluc, the French commander. Sliding under the fence, he managed, with the offer of only six packs of Camel cigarettes, to persuade the German subaltern in charge of the emplacement to shift it a quarter of a mile away. However, there was no way of communicating with the mortars set up in the woods around the camp. And so, during the night of April 15-16, when the English arrived at the village, a constant shower of German missiles flew over our heads. The English counterfire came closer and closer, and finally the French and Italian commands both gave orders for two men in every hut to mount constant guard. An important measure to insure that if any hut were blown to bits, the sleeping occupants would be immediately informed of what had hit them. Fortunately, the firing died down. Apparently, the English knew of the existence and locality of the camp and wanted to spare it. During the morning, there was a brisk battle inside the village, and by noon the German artillery also ceased fire. The silence was indeed golden.

That Crazy Major

Now let us go back to the afternoon of April 17, the day after the liberation, when the German troops made their unexpected return. Nothing in this world is a matter of sheer chance; one event always hinges upon another. An English armored unit had surrounded the village, but it was its own prisoner. Had men been dispersed to clean up the zone, the encirclement would have been broken and the Germans hiding in the woods would have been able to flee. Infantry detachments were supposed to be on the way, but infantrymen are the same in every army in the world (except in Germany, Japan and two other countries which shall, for political reasons, be nameless!). They always manage to miss the bus, and I don't blame them, because a civilized man can't be dead set on going to his death as quickly as possible.

This was why Major Cooley had undertaken the conquest of our camp with only two followers. It had happened, furthermore, that during the morning of April 17, on his way back from a second visit to the camp, the major met a German sergeant and, in a moment of weakness, shot him down. The sergeant, in spite of his Germanic mulishness, realized that with several bullets in his head it was no use to go on living and promptly expired. He chose a most inappropriate place to do so, just in front of the ovens where some Italian soldiers, with the encouragement of a little group of French officers, were baking bread. Someone told the Germans that their comrade was dead and they raided the bakery, spreading a hail of shot on the hastily abandoned ground floor and then accusing the miserable bakers, who had sought refuge in the attic, of murder. They were only half convinced of the innocent fellows' story; finally they sent them back to their huts and took the French officers with them as hostages. While they were hiding in the woods, the Germans had not known exactly what was going on in the camp, but their questioning of the French officers informed them.

The End of Captain Armistice

And so the Germans once more ruled over the camp. Some zealous citizens of the nearby village, including a big, blond boy who, as a faithful member of the *Hitler-jugend,* retained his confidence in a Nazi victory even at 5:15 P.M. of April 17, 1945, made it known that we had a cache of weapons which we had gathered up in the surrounding woods. The Germans were extremely courteous and logical about the choice with which they confronted us. Either we were to consider ourselves as still prisoners of war and hand over the men and weapons we had sequestrated, or else they would have to treat us as enemies and fire their machine guns against us.

Fortune is always on the side of the heavier battalions,

and so we had to give in. We handed over the small quantity of arms and freed our German hostages. There were quite a few of the latter, because wandering German soldiers had stumbled into the camp, looking for refuge. Our temporary captives had to resume their combat status, and I remember distinctly the sad look on their faces. After all, a German is better off in the hands of Frenchmen or Italians than in those of his fellow Germans. Even "Captain Armistice," with his knapsack over his shoulder, went off to the woods with the rest of them. He was accused of having failed to resist the English attack, and summarily hanged.

Captain Armistice is the only German toward whom I harbor any kindly feelings whatsoever. He was a good fellow, and I pray that God may forgive him for being born a German and provide a quiet spot in Purgatory for his benefit. Poor Captain Armistice! At this point, he's more likely Captain Last Judgment.

Pig-Headed People

April 18

When Major Cooley came back this morning he was amazed to find the French guards he had left at the gate disbanded. And when he was told what had been going on, he was more incredulous than ever. The village was ringed by English tanks, so that it was utterly ridiculous for the Germans to be lording it around as if, where they were concerned, the war weren't over.

Obviously the major had had little experience with Germans, or else they wouldn't have amazed him. Once I knew a German woman, who having lived for some years in Italy with an Italian husband, had learned to think straight, and this is a childhood story of the first world war which she told me.

"I was in primary school," she said, "and at least once a week, for the duration of the war, we found the school doors closed. 'Today's a holiday,' the janitor would tell us; 'we've won an important battle.' I particularly remember the two last holidays of this kind because one followed immediately upon the other. Tuesday, school was closed, because we had won a victory on the French front; Wednesday it was closed again, because we had lost the war."

That's the way of the Germans; they are so disciplined that if they have received orders to win a war, they'll go ahead and win it, right up to the second they have to backtrack, because the *Oberkommando* has sent orders to surrender.

And so the English major was first amazed and then angry; he went back to his tanks with highly belligerent intentions. Before he returned in the afternoon, he had notified the Germans that if they touched a hair of our heads they would be hanged immediately after capture.

"Revenge is a cowardly and barbarous affair," Arturo was saying. "If I were killed, I shouldn't want anyone to avenge me. I simply don't want to be killed. Anyhow,

I can't agree with the English major. I go along a hundred percent with the idea of hanging the Germans and yet, in a way, my idea is diametrically opposed to his. I'd string them up, all right, but before they'd touched a hair of our heads, not after."

Arturo's idea was shared by the whole lot of us, and by the Frenchmen as well, and so we all tried to bring the English major around to it. We even consented to a compromise: we were willing to give up hanging the Germans, as long as they were made prisoners.

"Just take it easy," said the major. "Until the infantry arrives, I can't round up all the German soldiers in the village. If I break my tank formation, some of them would surely get away."

We shouldn't have been too unhappy to get rid of them by letting them go. But the major insisted that it was his duty to restrain them and that he could not move an inch for this reason.

"Even if they were to machine-gun us," muttered the usual Anglophobe.

Alive, at Least in Parts

April 21

The English major failed to show up again, and German soldiers continued to buzz about the camp. Moreover, among the papers left by the former German command, there were notes to the effect that the poor, physically depleted internees should be spared the hardship of a transfer from one place to another in order to avoid falling into the "enemy's" hands. A bit of carefully planned machine-gunning, synchronized with a bombardment from the outside, would take care of them much more efficiently.

To find that you have survived by a miracle is obviously a source of satisfaction, that is, if you are quite sure of surviving. But on this score we still had considerable doubt; Germany often seemed to us to belong to another planet, because it was a land so totally foreign to our own. Our uncomfortable suspense lasted for three days thereafter.

Toward Liberty

April 22

All of a sudden we received orders to pack our knapsacks, leaving behind everything that was not strictly necessary. There had been ˙ negotiations between the Germans and the English major, leading up to a truce of several hours, sufficient for all French and Italian internees to reach the Allied lines. In other words, the Germans made a present of us to the Allies. Without knowing how or why, we found ourselves walking along a road with clumps of trees, scorched by flame-throwers and riddled by machine-gun fire, on either side, and a series of overturned cars and disemboweled tanks in the middle. We proceeded without an escort but with a Red Cross flag at our head. After two or three miles we went, undisturbed, by a German outpost, where heavy machine guns were still in view; a quarter of a mile farther on, we saw the first army trucks with a white star painted on the side.

Many of my comrades say that it was an extraordinary sight, enough to craze us with joy, but I simply don't remember. What did I think? Probably nothing at all. The only detail to stick in my mind was the Camel cigarette an American soldier had balanced on his ear. Before we left the camp, they had given each one of us a two-pound loaf of bread and a large tin of meat, which were to carry us through I don't remember how many days. I remember that, once I had thrown the pack of my belongings onto a truck, I sat down on the ground and devoured this whole stock of provisions. Every man thanks God the best way he can.

Then we went on walking. After some four or five miles we arrived, quite suddenly, in a town so immaculately neat that it seemed as if it must be brand new. For one thing, it was completely empty. Two days before, the inhabitants had been evacuated, each one taking no more than a suitcaseful of bare essentials with him.

"Every man's entirely on his own," we were told. "No use fighting over a place to sleep because there's plenty of room."

We were presented with an entire town on a silver platter; in many of the houses, the dining table was set, and there was steaming soup in a saucepan. In my own case, I opened a door and found myself face to face with 1,200 pounds of sugar.

It's Easy Enough to be a Gentleman on a Full Stomach

When it's a question of discovering among other peoples qualities lacking in their own, Italians are always ready. Throughout the centuries, this has been their attitude. Although neither Tacitus nor Livy says anything about it, we can be sure that in ancient Rome, even the fiercest opponents of Hannibal swore that, when it came to elephants, you had to take your hat off to the Carthaginians.

When they fought first the Turks and later the Abyssinians, Italians inevitably found in themselves a number of points of inferiority. And after, when as members of the Axis, they were sucked into the German war venture, the most anti-Nazi among them admitted at the drop of a hat that, where honest observance of rationing regulations was concerned, the Germans had it all over us. "Hoarders and black-marketeers," they insisted, "are typically Italian. In Germany it's a very different story; rich and poor, mighty and humble, all scrupulously observe the law. Hitler is a criminal and a madman, if you like, but he limits himself to his own ration coupons." They held so steadfastly to this opinion that the three thousand hungry Italian internees who entered the abandoned houses of Bergen had a terrible shock coming to them.

Here were sacks of flour, rice, sugar, coffee, boxes of canned goods of every description, barrels of salted meat and molasses, closets filled with wool suiting and even uncarded wool, hidden compartments in the walls stuffed with linens, safety pins, soap, neckties and spools of thread. Buried in the gardens vats of bacon, lard, honey, eggs and butter. Up in the attics, underneath the hayricks and woodpiles, jars of marmalade and cans of oil. And barns, barnyards and chicken coops packed with live chickens, geese, pigs, cows and calves.

Inspired by the noble urge of self-abasement, Italians had managed to feel inferior even to Germans, those people truly from another world, and now this illusion, in which they had cradled themselves for the four war years, collapsed and fell to the ground. Even in the field of rationing, Italians were no lower than Germans; in fact, they were a cut above them. But if Italians are easily dismayed, they rebound with equal facility. Quite naturally, "hunger had greater power than sorrow."

An English patrol was shocked to find an Italian captain sitting on the sidewalk of one of the central streets, plucking a chicken. But we must remember that it was a Nazi chicken and that, while it's easy enough to be a gentleman on a full stomach, it's a very different matter on one that for nineteen months has been empty. Under such conditions, the eternal battle between body and spirit is more ferocious than ever, and reason is often the loser. Ordinarily, a Ph.D. in literature would find a half-gallon of molasses totally repellent. But during our stay in Bergen, a high school teacher set his lips to the neck of a molasses bottle and did not take them off until it was empty. An artillery lieutenant found a big slab of margarine and ate it as if it were bread. Nor was he in the least discomfited when he found out that it was in reality a sort of camphorated grease used for massages.

After nineteen months of hunger, logic is at a low ebb. Because flour is a white powder, any white powder is taken for flour. Several fellows tried to make bread out of plaster. The plaster crumbled, but croquettes of meat, dipped in plaster flakes before frying, were acclaimed as crisp and delicious.

By Way of Reparation

The chicken population was speedily eliminated; indeed, in our haste, we as often as not neglected to remove the giblets before cooking. Once the chickens were gone, we had to turn to the pigs, and they were far less simple to deal with. To wring a chicken's neck is a comparatively easy matter, but to slaughter a pig is some-

thing else again. Among three thousand university grad-
uates, only three doctors and two veterinarians had the
remotest idea of how to go about it. For the overwhelm-
ing majority of us, chicken-killing was as far as we could
go. Beyond this apex of our culture lay nothing but
confusion and chaos.

It is not surprising, then, that various officers should
have misguidedly imagined that pigs were only outsize
chickens. When they were unable to wring their necks
they had an equally unsuccessful recourse to hanging.
In a barnyard some distance outside the town, I saw five
officers gathered around a hog, with the firm resolve of
sending it to its fathers. They began by clubbing it,
until another fellow arrived with a hammer. The miserable beast made an infernal noise, but betrayed no intention of giving up the ghost. Finally an exceedingly
pig-headed fellow went for a knife.

I can't find words with which to tell the rest of the
story. After a while, someone remembered that the knife
blow must strike the animal's heart. Because they were
unable to pick out the exact point of the hide on which
to place the fatal blow, they finally ripped open the
belly and found the organ they were looking for.

If any society for the prevention of cruelty to animals
feels like bringing suit against these war criminals, I
have their names in my possession. I have also the names
of three officers who, because they were unable to
slaughter a cow, simply cut beefsteaks out of its flanks.
But before the judge pronounces his sentence, he must

know what is to be shut up for nineteen months in a German internment camp.

Russian Cultural Discoveries

A few miles away from Bergen, in some former German army barracks, there was an improvised encampment of newly liberated Russians. I may open myself to the accusation of being "un-Italian," "reactionary," "neo-Fascist," "royalist," and the rest, but I intend to speak my mind. I have nothing in particular against the Russians, but they are foreigners, and all foreigners are the same. If I am allowed to say that the Chinese eat birds' nests, then surely I may state that the Russians drink eau de Cologne. Trustworthy persons have testified to the ways of the Chinese. As for the Russians, I have seen them with my own eyes, and I consider myself trustworthy.

The Heroics of Bicycling

If the Germans hadn't wasted their time making V-1's and V-2's, *Panzerfausten* and anti-tank weapons, and had concentrated on the manufacture of bicycles, the war might have come to quite a different end. I am firmly convinced that if they had strewn bicycles over the path of the Russian advance, the whole offensive would have been stalled.

After all I have heard and seen, I can't imagine a Russian catching sight of a bicycle without throwing himself lustfully upon it. When a Russian lays eyes on a bicycle he forgets everything except his desire to mount it and ride away. Before you can say Jack Robinson he is pedaling off at top speed. A few yards later he may be flat on the ground, but he remounts, falls off again, picks himself up and repeats the whole cycle ad infinitum.

Bombs may burst, mines explode and enemy counter-offensives encircle him, but not even an earthquake, flood, volcano eruption or eclipse of the sun would divert him from his intent. Until he has mastered the secret of keeping his balance on a two-wheeled vehicle, the heavens may fall without attracting his attention. Because he is a reasoning being, it is only a matter of time —six hours or thirty-six hours, as the case may be—until the secret is his.

After this, all the events which we have just named may recur, or new and graver ones may for the first time descend upon him, but nothing can distract his attention from the second phase, which we may call the enjoyment of success. Until his vehicle's front wheel comes up against a tree, wall, lamppost, automobile radiator or the belt of a tank, nothing in the world can obstruct our cyclist's progress. He has iron calf muscles, so that corduroy roads, plowed fields and meadows all stretch out smoothly before him. If ever he tumbles into a ditch, we may expect to see him pedal up the opposite bank, as triumphantly invulnerable as a tank.

Just Give Them Bicycles

Because the Russians aren't accustomed to bourgeois luxuries, they don't really notice whether or not a captured bicycle has any tires. The metal parts are all that count. If, for instance, there isn't a saddle, then a bundle of rags or a piece can be attached with a piece of wire or string to the frame and provide a perfectly adequate seating arrangement. From a certain point of view—neither political nor military—the greatest discovery that the Russians made in Germany was the bicycle.

It is easy to understand, then, that the Russians entered the town of Bergen in the guise of bicycle-hunters. They made a thorough search of rooms, attics, cellars and other possible hiding places. Actually, they were content to find mere parts—handlebars, brakes, pedals or even bells, which they proceeded to weld into highly original composite vehicles. Quite a lot of them didn't function, for lack of a chain, a fork, or even a wheel, but, in bicycling, as well as in other fields, where there's a will there's a way. A Russian who had obtained no more than a single pedal gave himself the airs of an accomplished cyclist, and every time he had to go anywhere, he rolled up his trouser legs, as if to protect them from the chain he hoped to possess one day. Whenever we saw a Russian with his trouser legs turned normally down, we could be sure he expected to find a bicycle complete with a chain housing.

Russians Have an Eye for Style

Three hours after the Russians had entered Bergen every single bicycle part in the town had been brought to the light of day. After this the visitors turned their attention to the problem of clothing. The problem was an urgent one, because after so many months of imprisonment, the poor fellows were really in a bad way. As long as they confined themselves to laying aside their filthy rags in favor of the well-stocked wardrobes of the fugitive Germans, we looked benevolently on their efforts. But when they had exhausted the German stores, they directed a roving eye at our knapsacks, and this was a different story. They vaulted through the windows and fastened their admiring gaze upon a pair of boots, a shirt or a sweater. In answer to our protest, they uttered the single word *"Deutsch,"* to signify that whatever they might lay their hands on was German booty. It was wiser not to argue about it, for although a single Russian is as much of a human being as anyone else, a group of Russians is intractable to the highest degree. A Russian alone may smile and call you *"Kamerad,"* but in the company of his fellows, he is more likely to frown and even address you as a "dirty Fascist," if you refuse to hand over your trousers.

We Westerners have a mistaken notion of Russian taste. Propaganda has painted Communism as a brutally leveling force, destructive of personality and leaving nothing but a mass of robots behind it. We cannot detach the individual from the collectivity, but imagine him as one of an identical series, clad in the stereotype cap, blouse and high boots.

Because the only word of their language I knew was 'harosho, and this was no basis for conversation, I am unable to pass judgment on the contemporary Russian soul. But as far as Russian esthetics are concerned, I can testify that most Westerners have a radically wrong idea. In their taste for clothes, Russians are highly individualistic, and the styles they go for are, to say the least, original.

Models All Their Own

I saw one Russian wearing a well-cut, double-breasted, pin-striped suit, together with a sailor's cap and a turtleneck sweater. Another son of the steppes wore a pale blue sport jacket over a pair of tuxedo trousers, and on his head a red cloth fancy-dress-party hat, with a white feather.

The Germans, no matter how rudely they jostle the living, show eminent respect for the dead. Even your mere peasant has a long-tailed coat with satin lapels and a shiny top hat which he mournfully dons for a family funeral. So that when a fashion-crazy Russian came to a house occupied by some of my good-natured companions, it was perfectly easy to satisfy him. They rigged him up in a top hat too large for his shaven pate, and it fell at intervals over his forehead, submerging him in darkness, and in a modish blue-and-white striped jersey, which took the place of a shirt. When he was faced by the tailcoat, the good fellow almost lost his head completely, but with the brotherly aid of his new Italian friends he was soon in proper funeral attire. He gazed contentedly into a mirror, dazzled by the contrast between the shiny satin lapels of the coat and the blue-and-white stripes of the jersey. All he needed was a collar and tie, and it was quite a job to contrive them. Finally, however, by means of a dozen safety pins, a stiff collar was attached to the jersey and set off by a bright green tie. One practical joker tried to persuade him to hang an alarm clock around his neck, but the good *moujik* said no, and went off bearing it in his pocket.

All this goes to show that, no matter how eccentric these Russians may be, they have a certain sense of restraint and proportion.

The Usual Watch-and-Clock Story

Apropos of clocks, there is something more I should like to say. I've heard all too many eye witness accounts and read all too many stories, in French, Swiss and Italian papers, about the Russian mania for clocks and watches. The idea has found currency that to the Russians, all timepieces have something mythical and supernatural about them.

This I don't deny, but I insist that the Russians are not the only watch-lovers. During my two years in various camps I rubbed up against many hundreds of Russians, Poles, Czechoslovaks, Yugoslavs, Greeks, Bulgarians, Frenchmen, Englishmen and Americans, and all of them seemed to feel the same way, including the Allied soldiers who came to liberate us. And what about the Germans? The Germans were incorruptible, that is, up to the point where you showed them a watch. At Beniaminovo a German soldier walked into one of the huts and found Lieutenant Lombardi's quite illegal radio going full blast. The discovery should have been fatal, but unfortunately Lombardi still had his watch upon him. When he held it out, the German muttered a few incomprehensible words, then snatched it and ran away, leaving the radio behind him.

Let us puncture the myth of the watches. All I can say is this: the Russians like wall clocks and alarm clocks just as well. I saw one going back to his encampment with an enormous grandfather clock grasped lovingly in his arms. The clock had chimes, and when all of a sudden music poured forth the fellow stopped in his tracks and listened ecstatically. I never go out on a limb, but in this case I'd be willing to bet that he got it all the way back to his *isbah*.

Here is something else that I saw. A Russian with a most unprepossessing face entered a house, pocketed an alarm clock and went away. Before he reached the garden gate the alarm went off, and he at once took the clock out of his pocket, hurled it onto the ground and killed it with pistol shots. Here I'm not betting anything. For if I were to swear that I'd seen it with my own eyes, I'd be sent to an oculist. Russia occupies a considerable part of the earth's surface; some of its people live in isolation, like shipwreck escapees on a desert island. So I don't say that all Russians kill alarm clocks; I simply state that I saw one in the act of so doing. Perhaps he was the only one out of all Russia, and fate willed that I should be there to see. What harm is there in killing a clock, anyhow? There are madmen the world over.

I like Russians. Consider this one, for instance, who took up his abode in a sort of shack across the way from the villa where some of my friends had their quarters.

"I'm waiting here," he told them, "until you go away. Then I shall burn down the house in which you are now living. The Germans murdered my wife and children, burned my house and then beat me up and made me work like a mule for two years in this very place. I have every right to destroy it."

I really shouldn't go on about the Russians this way. Once I got home, I meant never to speak of them again. But back in my own town, I saw on the window of a No. 8 trolley a sticker that read: "When Stalin comes, he'll see that everyone has a job." No. 8 is the trolley I ride every day, and after I'd read this two, four, six, a dozen times, it began to get on my nerves.

EPILOGUE

My Dear Reader:

Perhaps you will find what you read in the following pages a bit unexpected. Twelve years have passed between the page you have just turned and this one here. This year I went back as a free man over the same route I had been forced to take as a prisoner. And just as I had kept a secret diary in the past, now I have written down the thoughts that came to me along the way. And so you too must change your sights from the barbed wire limits of a *Lager* to the ever widening boundaries of Europe, of a Europe moving toward unity in spite of the innumerable bureaucratic barriers in a world where many people have memories similar to those I recorded in secret.

For me and perhaps for many of you what follows is an epilogue. But what there is of faith and hope in these pages will make of it a prologue for your sons and mine. But now I write as if I were a wise old man. It's not true! My mustache is as black as ever.

1. Albertino and I Go Back

Of the many possible routes from the Garoda to the mouth of the Elba, that which passes through Trieste is undoubtedly the most ill-advised. The Elba, of course, is a river that crosses Germany from southeast to northwest, running through Dresden, Madgeburg and Hamburg, on its way to the North Sea. And the Garoda is a canal—little more than a ditch—which runs from south to north through my infinitesimally small village of Le Roncole, between Parma and Cremona, into another canal of the same dimensions, bordering the west side of the piece of land where I have set up my descendants' ancestral home.

Yes, I have chosen the longest possible route between my village and the marshland which extends from the mouth of the Elba to that of the Weser, and for this reason. Fourteen years ago, when I was transported thither, I crossed the border at the city of Tarviso.

In September of 1943 my prisoner's knapsack contained not only a miserable miscellany of everything I had been able to gather up from the Citadel of Alessandria, but also a cargo of hopes and illusions. Today I carry a suitcase full of shirts, undershirts, shorts, socks, handkerchiefs, and so on.

Prosperity. Everyone's talking about prosperity. But a miserable knapsack swung over the shoulder may be less of a burden than a prosperous suitcase carried in the trunk of a streamlined car. The time has come when the general prosperity reminds me of my spiritual dearth. I'd gladly throw away the contents of my handsome suitcase in exchange for the knapsack I carried fourteen years ago, loaded with miscellaneous objects, with hunger and faith.

I want to go back to that northern clime, to walk once more the sand that I trod in a pair of prisoner's wooden shoes. I want to go back, as a free man, over the road which I first took in a freightcar. I first saw Germany through a freightcar's boarding, then, in an internment camp, I came to know its raw air and angry sky. For a brief time my captors were no longer German but English, and I saw Germany fall to pieces. Eventually, the English liberators turned me over to Italian liberators, and from then on I followed Germany's resurgent fortunes from afar.

I shall go back to the *Lager* not simply to steep myself in pains gone by, but as an Italian who, having day by day lost more of his strictly Italian faith, wants to strengthen the faith he would like to have as a European. In the name of a free and United Europe I should like to bury, alongside the remains of my comrades who died in captivity, all memory of my own suffering and all personal resentment.

Everything is ready in the new car: a big suitcase, an overnight bag, a typewriter, two cameras, and one Albertino. The last-named is undoubtedly the most cumbersome piece of baggage of all, since although he's less bulky than I, he's nearly six feet tall. It's good to have him along, however, because his eyes haven't seen the same sad things as mine, and for that reason they are bright, serene and open to new impressions, which will serve to check mine.

When I was a prisoner, I summoned up Albertino three times in my imagination, across the miles and through the barbed-wire enclosure. Once, when he was only three years old, the poor fellow had to come in his nightshirt, leading his newborn baby sister by the hand, and introduce her to me. And so, this trip is a payment, made to the flesh-and-blood Albertino, of a debt I have long owed to his ethereal, imaginary counterpart.

Margherita watches over the process of loading and embarkation. She has no particular advice to give me, and as for her son, she has already given him all it is possible for one human being to give another. Even so, just as I am starting the motor, she calls out:

"Be careful when you cross the frontier!"

I slip into low and then second gear.

"*Aufwiedersehen*, Margherita!"

In my briefcase, beside some faithful bicarbonate of soda and a large supply of pills, there are the greasy notebooks, in which from September 8, 1943 to August 28, 1945, I recorded, day by day, everything that happened to my comrades and myself and my ensuing reflections.

It is an overly detailed, tedious diary, but it serves me now to rediscover the frame of mind in which I arrived at Tarvisio, fourteen years ago. We still have a long way to go, and so I ask Albertino to take out notebook number one and read from it out loud.

"Start with our departure from Alessandria, and go on until I tell you to stop."

While I drive carefully over the wet asphalt, result of a steady drizzle of rain, Albertino reads:

September 13. Monday.

We managed to cook something but we had no time to sit down at the table. Carrying our baggage (if we had any) on our backs we went to assemble in the courtyard. The German lieutenant sent around a paper saying in both German and Italian: "I swear to give my last drop of blood for the German Reich and the triumph of the new Europe . . ."

Albertino pauses to exclaim in astonishment:
"Were they already talking about a New Europe in those times?"
"Yes," I explain, "but Hitler's idea had nothing to do with the New Europe which free Europeans are trying to bring about today."
Albertino reads on:

It was just a matter of signing the paper. Those Italian officers and soldiers who didn't sign were to be taken off in ten minutes to internment in Germany. Two trucks, with their motors going, waited outside.

A bunch of us climbed into the trucks, while our comrades called out that they'd join us on the next trip. The trucks unloaded us at the station and then started back to the barracks, but we never saw them again.

This time I was the one to interrupt:
"Later on, when we were moved from camp to camp, we traveled for hundreds of miles in sealed freightcars. But for this trip from Alessandria to Bremervörde we did go in conventional carriages, which stayed in Germany to work for the greatness of the Reich."

At Verona we stopped between a freight train overflowing with Italian soldiers, and another, whose open cars were packed with Slavs being moved to Germany from an internment camp at Padua. The Italian soldiers stared at us without speaking, except for a corporal, by his accent obviously from Rome, who called out sarcastically: "You officers, there, all you ever thought about was the polish on your shoes . . . !"

The Slavs hated us just as much, but in silence. One of them finally did speak, upon our solicitation, and then only in order to give us some purely technical pointers. "You'll be hungry for the first few months; after that, you'll get used to it."

Albertino wants to know if this is true. But I tell him that it isn't. Even after a year and a half, every day's hunger seemed like something new.

Trains teeming with humanity arrived, while others went away. In place of the trainload of Italians, there followed a convoy of English prisoners. We had some extra bread and offered it to them, but they wanted only chocolate. After dark, they began singing, "Tipperary," and their good cheer may have been quite justified, because the young German sergeant who was in charge of us said that within a few months the war would be over and *"Deutschland kaput."*

September 15. Wednesday.
There were people assembled in front of every house close to the railroad tracks and at every grade crossing. They had come to say goodbye to their deported

brothers. Old women dressed in black, whose sons had
died in the Julia Division, threw out their arms as we
passed by. This gesture and their tearful eyes seemed
to reflect endless despair. All the way to the province
of Veneto, we had met with complete indifference or
hatred, but here, in the extreme northeastern corner
of Italy, we breathed a truly Christian and human
air. Here we were not "You officers," the sons of ex-
ploiters and profiteers, but brothers on the way to
exile. Train after train of prisoners must have come
this way, but still the local population continued to
offer some comfort. They insisted upon giving us
bread, apples and all they had left of tobacco. At Ba-
siliano a woman with a tub full of water ran along
the platform from one end of the train to the other
and if anyone had a handkerchief or an undershirt
to be washed, she managed to wash it before the train
went on. Her zeal and speed were positively heart-
breaking.

At Udine a little boy handed me a piece of ice
through the window, and in spite of his small size he
accompanied it with these unforgettable words:
"We're all the same people." When the train moved,
the stationmaster, an old man with a white mustache,
drew himself up to attention and raised one hand to
his cap in salute . . .

September 16. Thursday.
Travelling this way, in an Italian railway carriage,
we had no idea of the distance we were covering. Even

after we had been through a dozen foreign cities, we
should not have been surprised to see the familiar
outlines of Milan or Bologna. As we proceeded toward
Salzburg, the green fields and flowering gardens of
this section of Austria were not too unlike what we
were accustomed to at home.

Enough of my diary!

It is dark and still rainy by the time we arrive at the
frontier post of Tarvisio, but once more, Austria gives
us a propitious welcome. The Austrian garrison and customs office is meagerly manned in comparison with its
Italian counterpart. One man in uniform and another
in civilian clothes, with a conspicuous patch on the lapel
of his overcoat, are the only ones to await us.

The civilian looks at me askance because, before getting out to exhibit our passports, I forgot to put on the
handbrake (mechanics have always been beyond me!),
and the car takes advantage of the downward slope to
stretch its legs and roll forward. Albertino remedied the
situation before it has rolled more than six inches, but
the civilian official is supremely irritated, as I can tell
from the mere sound of his voice. But all of a sudden he
stares first at me and then at my passport and gaily exclaims: *"Don Camillo und Peppone!"*

We take leave of each other as the best of friends, and
I step on the accelerator with all the more pleasure,
inasmuch as Albertino has not yet taken it in. Many
times in the course of our trip he is to see people exam-
ine my handlebar mustache and then cry out: *"Don Ca-*

millo und Peppone!" Reluctantly, he has to admit that, at least abroad, his father is a highly respected person.

The goal of our journey is not Austria. We have come this way simply because it was our prisoners' itinerary fourteen years ago. The next step is to drive to Munich. Only a few miles on the highway will take us to the German frontier.

"Shall I read some more from your diary?" asks Albertino.

"Yes, go ahead and read."

Notebook number one is quickly found.

September 17. Friday.

After Salzburg, the landscape changed. Behind the bars of a grade crossing, five little boys in brown shirts with a red armband and a swastika watched us go by. All together they made an eloquent gesture signifying that they would just as soon cut our throats. "We must be in Germany," said one of my Italian friends.

I interrupt Albertino and tell him to put the notebook back in the briefcase. We go on for several miles without his saying a word. Then at last he says:

"Those boys would be grownup by now. They'd be twenty-three or -four years old."

"Yes, if they weren't burned or crushed to death in an air raid," I answer. That is all I have to say. Germany is waiting.

2. Germany

Accustomed as he is to fighting every day with plain-clothes officials who try to complicate the simplest things, and with uniformed ones who treat every citizen as a criminal in disguise, your average Italian cannot but feel let down when he crosses the Austrian border. With just a glance at his passport, the Austrian customs guard waves him on. It's all too easy, and he is cheated of the feeling of triumphant achievement.

But the German customs give him greater satisfaction. First of all, they not only scrutinize his passport, but they check his name against a list of undesirable individuals, and this gives him a pleasurable shiver. If he hasn't the proper entrance permit for his car, then he must secure a temporary one from another office, and if necessary a 16-mark a week insurance policy. It's not very bad, because the guards are perfectly polite and don't even ask to open the trunk on the back of the car, but it's enough to give the average person the impression that he's really somebody, after all. Because I respond in this very average way, I heave a sigh of relief when the frontier post is behind me and say:

"Thank God, we made it!"

"Why do you say that?" asks Albertino suspiciously.

I tell him that I'm thankful we didn't have to wait in line, as is often necessary at places of this sort, but got through the formalities in no more than a few minutes. This little lie is simply because I can't very well explain that your typical Italian, even when he is at rest with his conscience and in good standing with the law, can't help praising the Lord every time he passes successfully through a bureaucratic blockade.

At a certain point along the way, we pick up a hitch-hiker. He is a young engineering student, who speaks some Italian, since he recently traveled, by this same system, through Italy during his summer vacation. I ask him the question which I intend to address to as many Germans as can understand me:

"In the years since 1900, Italians have made a reputation for themselves in every field of endeavor. Tell me the first three Italian names that come to your mind."

This young man answers, unhesitatingly:

"Caruso, Toscanini, Gigli."

My innocent little question turns out to be loaded with dynamite. At Wolfsburg, a Volkswagen executive votes for Sophia Loren, De Sica and some unspecified Jesuit. But don't let's put the cart before the horse. Germany is waiting . . .

To me, the face of the new Germany is represented not by the Prussian frown but by the Bavarian smile. In respect to the future of all of us, the most important governmental unit is the Ministry of War, or rather Defense, the *Bundeministerium fur Verteidung*. Not only does this ministry have its offices in Bavaria, but the ministry itself is Bavarian as well. I don't mean that all the employees, high and low, are Bavarian, but that there is a Bavarian feeling in the air.

What do the Germans think of unification? Is it possible for them to give up the idea? Is it likely that, as German economic and military efficiency are restored, the Germans will return to talking about *Lebensraum,* or space to expand in? These are the uncertainties which keep many peaceful people awake at night.

It is not easy to give definite answers, and quite impossible to say what the Germans are thinking. By Germans, I mean the majority of those who owe allegiance to the Republic of Bonn, and who are represented by it. All I can report is what the Germans *say* they are thinking. Because I'm not one of those newspaper writers that is at the same time a political expert, I can't say for sure what goes on inside their heads.

Conservative Germans seem to me to hold very sensible views on the subject of unification. They want it, to be sure, but they are dead against the idea of wanting it "at any cost" and "right away." It is plain to them that such slogans come straight out of the fertile brain of Khrushchev.

But they do not, for this reason, give up their ideal or wait for it to come about through divine intervention. They are working with stubborn intelligence to balance the excess of Soviet power with a powerful United Europe, within the orbit of the Atlantic Union. Because their national unification cannot be achieved for the moment, they regard European unity as all the more essential. For other people, beginning with the majority of Italians, European unity is a mere catchword, but the Germans take it seriously.

To wait for the unification of their own country does not discomfit them. In the "island" of Berlin there are three million Germans who will never favor Russia, and in East Germany anti-Russian feeling is bound to grow and grow. The Russians themselves will see to that.

Bonn, formerly a noble and quiet city on the banks of the Rhine, with a population of pensioners and other old people, was suddenly raised to the position of capital of West Germany. But Bonn did not lose its head; it continued to go its own quiet way. The population increased, but, here is the amazing thing, it increased only by the exact number of government employees and their families who were transferred thither. The city was *not* invaded by crowds of lobbyists and experts in the field of obtaining governmental favors. Bonn is still the simple honest place that it was before, with the addition of twenty-two ministries. For this reason it is eminently fitted to be the capital of the new serene and hard-working Germany and for my part I do not hesitate to recommend it as the spiritual capital of the United Europe to which we all aspire.

Bonn is laid out on a very simple plan. I have an appointment at the Ministry of Defense at five o'clock in the afternoon, and the building is only two or three hundred yards from my hotel. Unfortunately, it is raining, and still more unfortunately, I decide to go over there in my car. In order to keep my five o'clock appointment, I leave at half-past four, but at half-past five

I find myself, under a pouring rain, on the road to Coblenz. Finally I make my way back to Bonn, but not having the nerve to go see the Minister at this late hour I return shamefully to my hotel. The only thing for me to do is to leave town this evening and not show my face again.

At half-past six, I am packing my suitcase, when the telephone rings and an agreeable woman secretary's voice tells me that when the Minister had her ring me earlier in the afternoon my son reported me on the way to pay my call. By now, while Albertino is presumably scouring the city to find me, the Defense Minister has reluctantly decided to go home. The kindly secretary goes on to say, in excellent Italian, that he congratulates me upon my safe return to the hotel and hopes to see me at nine o'clock the next morning. But, for safety's sake, he hopes that I will take a taxi. My heart is warmed by so much understanding, and I am reborn, as a citizen of both Italy and a United Europe as well.

These people have understood what sort of a fellow I am, and when I reach the building which I presume is the seat of the Ministry of Defense, another pleasant individual appears at the top of the steps and beckons to me as if to say that this is indeed the place for which I am looking. The place is most wonderfully lacking in bureaucratic flavor, and none of the persons who greet me on my way has that stereotyped governmental manner. But my heart beats faster, simply because the man I am going to see, whatever you may call him, is a Minister of War. Well, isn't he a man just like any other?

But there are reasons for my rather special state of mind. I am a former prisoner or internee; for nineteen months the lowliest German sergeant had power of life or death over me; I approached him with fear, because I knew that at any moment he might beat me or even shoot me down. Now, in spite of the intervening years and the changes they have brought with them, I still have something of a prisoner complex, and the prospect of appearing before a German Minister of War is obviously disturbing. Especially, when I kept him waiting for over an hour the day before!

But as soon as I set foot in the Minister's private office, my subconscious fear is allayed. Franz Josef Strauss is a man like any other, after all, in fact much more cordial and welcoming than most men I know. No matter how hard I strain my imagination, I simply cannot visualize him with a German army officer's cap on his head. I am happy to think that the face of the new Germany is that of the smiling and affable Strauss. The interpreter cannot read my thoughts, and this is just as well, because some things are better left unspoken. As he translates my opening words, I reflect that a prisoner of war, like myself, has a right to a certain satisfaction over being in my shoes. It is almost impossible, at this point, to remember my internment camp days. They seem a bad dream of a hundred years ago.

3. Men and Machines

Once I have freed myself from my prisoner-of-war complex, I have another one to deal with, which I shall call my "Prince-of-Wales complex." And this is a more serious matter. Strauss's smile may cause me to forget that I was once in a German internment camp, but not even a smile from Chancellor Adenauer (granting the man knows how to smile) could free me from acute consciousness of my four-button jacket.

Of course when I move around strictly as a private citizen, I am under no obligations as to what I should wear. But if I am traveling on public business of any kind, I can't very well look like a horsetrader. I trust the phrase "public business" is not misleading. I am not an official or representative person, but even if I represent myself and myself alone, I have to make certain distinctions. It is one thing if I am summoned to put in an appearance, as a notorious political backslider, before an Italian court, another if I go to cool off on the shores of a Swiss lake, another still if I take myself and my well-known mustache to participate in a charity all-star night in Paris.

In Italy, and even more abroad, there are people who still claim to have got fun out of reading certain stories I wrote several eons ago about Don Camillo or seeing the moving-pictures made out of them. Fortunately, there are only a few million of these deluded souls, but they are sufficient to have given my handlebar mustache the reputation of being highly picturesque and to have landed it in a number of weekly comic papers. Hence the necessity of presenting myself before the public in sober, well-cut garb, and the decision to glorify my heretofore neglected wardrobe with a four-button "Prince-of-Wales" suit.

Nine years have gone by since for the first time I abandoned my rustic bark and fitted myself into this decorous garment. I have worn it on more than one occasion since, but every time with the feeling of entering into another man's skin. The material is light and soft, the tailoring is beyond reproach, and yet it weighs as heavily upon me as if it were lined with lead. My discomfort is not merely physical, but mental as well. I feel oppressed to the point where I have to struggle to hold on to my old self and my old way of thinking.

The suit has a strong personality, which it is trying to impose upon me. It wants me to adapt myself, to be nothing more than the worthy contents of a fashionable, four-button, Prince-of-Wales suit. Every time I put it on, the same thing happens: each one of us tries to dominate the other. And at the end of the battle things are just the same as they were before. The suit is a fashionable, four-button, Prince-of-Wales model, which has landed by mistake on a rustic lout, and I am a rustic lout, who has accidentally fallen into a fashionable, four-button, Prince-of-Wales suit. We cordially dislike each other, but whenever "public business" is at hand, we travel together. For both of us are slaves to duty. Now, too, I am wearing this armor, and as it sits before the German

Minister of Defense, I must admit that it cuts a brave figure.

Once I have got a complete grip on myself, I tell Mr. Strauss that I am not sorry to have missed yesterday's appointment, because this mischance taught me that a democratic atmosphere has pervaded even the government offices of West Germany.

Then I go on to say that, having set out to become acquainted with the Germany of today, I cannot hope to learn from any more authoritative person than himself what are the guiding principles of the instruction imparted to the youngest generation of German soldiers. Of course, there is no need for me to say that Germany is famous for its military tradition. The Minister knows that better than I.

"No people can depart entirely from its traditions," he says at the very start, "even if these traditions have their dark side."

In other words, Germany does not renege its military tradition, but only its darker side. The dark side of Prussian "militarism" was the fact that the soldier was considered only an anonymous cog in the machine. In the new German army, on the contrary, he is treated like an individual.

Of course, mechanized war leaves little place for individual action; it demands, rather, that the single soldier become a member of a team. This implies a mortification of personality similar to that which we see in industry, where the worker must immolate himself to the machine. In army life, the soldier must be trained not only to submit to team discipline but at the same time to preserve a personality of his own. When he is serving as crew member of a tank, a bomber or an artillery battery, he must behave like a worker on an assembly line. But the rest of the time he is a man and an individual, with a face, a brain and a conscience of his own. The authority of his instructor must derive not from mere rank, but from proven ability. The instructor must be guided not by tradition alone, but also by the social changes of the last few decades. No longer can he operate in a realm of abstraction.

"The day is past when a man is forbidden to be more intelligent than his superior." And, with a laugh, he tells me the story of the green recruit who, after six weeks of basic training, says to his sergeant: "If that's all you have to teach us, you may as well stop right there. We know these things for ourselves."

At this point I can see, behind Strauss's back, the truculent face of the Prussian general whose face I so often saw, as a boy, in the pages of the illustrated weekly *Domenica del Corriere*. He is scowling even more ferociously than he did then, with a pointed steel helmet on his head and rays of lightning flashing out of the point. But I find no reason for his indignation. "No people can depart entirely from its traditions," the Minister said. From a back road I had seen a group of German recruits whose drilling was such as to win the applause of a dozen Prussian generals. As for Mr. Strauss, he has ideas to which I subscribe unconditionally.

"Ours is an age of radar, atomic power and automation. If we are to prevent man from being transformed into a robot, we must develop his individual capacities. This, and the world situation, are two factors of which we must take account in military training. To-day, war is a total affair. The world is divided into two opposing blocs, and we must train the soldier not only to defend his country from attack, but also to man his own soul against subversive psychological infiltration."

I remark that in Italy this holds even more true. For our Communist Party has not been banned, as in West Germany, but exists on an equal footing with the democratic groupings.

"If Italy were, most unfortunately, obliged to defend itself against Soviet aggression, do you think Italian Communists would support its defense effort?" Strauss asks.

"Only in part," I reply. "Only pseudo-Communists, like my village mayor, Peppone, would defend Italy. Those who have been schooled in Party doctrine would aid and abet the invader."

Then Mr. Strauss tells me that an Italian political figure who visited Bonn—whether officially or unofficially, I do not know—several years back, said that the author of *Don Camillo* was a highly untrustworthy individual.

"A crypto-Communist, that's what he called you." And we laugh together, before I ask my next-to-last question.

"Mr. Strauss, many Italians, looking back to the 'Rome-Berlin Axis' of Fascist days, wonder whether the two Christian Democrat parties may not construct a 'Rome-Bonn Axis' of the same kind."

To this Mr. Strauss makes a categorical answer.

"Impossible, because it is contrary to the idea of a United Europe. The bonds between Italy and Germany are much stronger and more sincere than they were in the 'Axis' days. But, to be quite frank, any attempt on our part to build up another alliance of this sort would damage our prospects of drawing closer to France. For the activation of his foreign policy, Chancellor Adenauer counts upon the support of the whole German people; in the field of economics, he relies upon the liberal policy of Ehrard. Our government is not a confessional one."

As the minister is bidding me goodbye, I shoot my last question at him.

"In the years since 1900, Italians have made a reputation for themselves in every field of endeavor. Tell me the first three Italian names that come to your mind."

The Minister gets off to a good start:

"Marconi, De Gasperi . . ." but then he has a moment of hesitation.

"And . . ."

"I can't decide between Gina Lollobrigida and Sophia Loren . . ."

It is with deep disappointment in my heart that I go away! My dear Minister of Defense, you can't possibly build a United Europe with such confusion in your head! The first step we must take is to banish pretense

and hypocrisy. We must look one another in the eye
and learn to know one another.

As I listened to you talk, I thought I had met a man
with definite ideas, but at the last minute you let me
down. You are clear-headed enough, in everything but
essentials. Your indecision between Gina and Sophia is
more than I can bear. If you had said you were hesitat-
ing between Caruso and Bartali, a singer and a bicycle
racer, who have no connections whatsoever, I might
have been able to understand. But now . . .

"Sophia, Mr. Strauss, Sophia!"

The man who stands before you is a good husband
and father, thrifty, laborious and far too dignified to let
any nonsense be put over on him. As a writer, he has
never penned an unclean word; frivolity is definitely
not his line. And yet when the radio reporter at Wolfsburg asked me to name the three most beautiful women
in the world, I said unhesitatingly:

"Sophia Loren, from the front, Sophia Loren from
the side, Sophia Loren from the rear."

And I went on my journey, holding my head high and
unashamed.

4. Sentimental Interlude

At Bremervörde, the heart of the sandy area between
the mouth of the Weser and that of the Elba, I at last
rediscover the Germany I once knew. It was at the sta-

tion of this town that we internees ended the journey
which we had begun at Alessandria at half-past five
o'clock in the afternoon of September 13, 1943. Here
we left our Italian railway carriages, the last remnants
of our native country and set out, with our knapsacks
on our backs, to tread the soil of a foreign land.

How long they were, those seven miles we covered on
that September 18! . . . There is the little cemetery,
where we were told we could sit down for a ten-minute
rest, and I remember distinctly that, near one of the
graves a woman was knitting a red sweater while a fair-
haired little girl played at her feet. German cemeteries,
at least those in the country, are not, like ours, shut in
by a high wall. There is no fear that the dead may rise
out of their tombs, and they are left free to enjoy the
fresh air and sun, with no more than a low fence or a
narrow surrounding ditch to guard them. From the
road you see what looks like a garden or an orchard,
and all the time it is a cemetery.

At Sandbostel, I rediscover the air, the sky, the general desolation of that September. The roads are deserted, just as they were then, and the houses, with their
moss-covered roofs, set among moss-covered trees, are
as empty as they were before. Everything is dripping
with rain, and the road is muddy.

Lager. There can be no mistaking the location, for an
enormous sign points the way. After crossing over two
narrow wooden bridges, we start to drive over the last
stretch of washed-clean, irregularly brick-paved road.
The camp buildings are just the same, long and low-

lying, as if they were crushed by the somber, overhanging sky. The only new feature is a small masonry church. In the old days, it could not have existed, for God was barely tolerated and had no right to an office within the camp enclosure.

The *Lager* of Sandbostel is still a going concern; it serves now as a camp for refugees. The grounds have been cleaned up and altered; it is hard to imagine that they were formerly ringed by a barbed-wire fence, complete with watchtowers and searchlights and armed guards ready to train a machine gun on an escapee. I see no way of recovering the thoughts I harbored then; it is quite hopeless to search for the other Giovannino. I am as ill at ease as if I had been forcibly ejected from a place that was once my home.

Back in the village I fall into conversation with a little man who is raking some wet grass. During the war he served in France, and now in bad French he points to the road leading to the prisoners' burying ground and asks me for a *Caporal* cigarette. I have nothing but half a pack of ordinary Italian cigarettes, which he accepts only upon assurance that they are no better than the French ones he once knew.

Albertino is alarmed by the sight of the road that lies ahead, deeply rutted and punctuated with mud holes and puddles.

"The car will sink down halfway up the wheels; we'll be stuck and never get out," is his opinion.

But I am not worried, for I know this terrain. It is prevalently sand, and what looks like mud doesn't stick to either shoes or wheels, because no sooner has it formed than it crumbles. Silence and melancholy are all around. A big black-and-white cow stares at me in hostile fashion. She has an ungainly, big head and a body as massive as that of a tractor. It seems as if she had emerged not from a stable but from a Krupp factory.

The little cemetery has undergone changes which have brought its atmosphere into line with the idea of European unity. It has been beautified by a wrought-iron gate, swinging between two stone pillars, and at a widened point of the central alley there is a great round, stone vase, with three columns which bear on them the words: *"Unsere Verpflichtung: Friede Europas."*

"What does it mean?" asks Albertino.

"It means: 'Be careful what you say; don't let these poor fellows know that their sacrifice was made in vain, and the world is more disgusting than it was before. May they rest in peace, in the illusion that they taught wisdom to those that came after.' "

"Does it really say that?"

"I don't know. That's what it says to me, and I'm satisfied."

Albertino is ready to take this for an answer. What he can't understand is why, on such a large plot of ground, there should be so few crosses. I explain that the large green patches that we see around us are not, as they seem, pine-tree nurseries, but graves.

"Under those young saplings are the mass-burial tombs where lie the bodies of those who died in large groups, either shot down or else felled by something like a typhus epidemic."

I tell Albertino to wander about in search of a good place from which to snap a picture, and I linger alone among the graves. I have been asked to find the grave of one of my former comrades and photograph it, and having located the Italian area, I proceed to scan the names inscribed on the crosses. There are not so many of them, but on the dark wood they are difficult to decipher.

"It's in the second row," says a voice from behind me.

Looking around, I see the raggedly clad Giovannino whom I came to seek in this desolate place.

"Second row, fourth cross on the lefthand side," he continues. "Why don't you take photographs of the others, too, while there's still time? The wood is rotting and the vegetation constantly growing. Within a few years this whole area will be wooded, and not even the slightest trace of these unfortunate fellows will remain."

I remark that he seems to be filled with bitterness, but he shakes his head in denial.

"They're really dead," he explains. "Deader, for instance, than that bearded old man who was run over by a trolley-car in your village some years ago. There are still people who remember the old man: the motorman, who saw him fall under the wheels, the policeman who drew up an on-the-spot report of the incident, the baker's delivery boy, who stopped to see what was going on. But these fellows, who's to remember them except their immediate families and some of their fellow-prisoners? Otherwise they're forgotten. Every one of their graves might as well be marked like that one: '*Unbekannt Ausland Soldat,* Unknown Foreign Soldier.' For twelve years, Giovannino, I've wandered about this place, trying to talk to them, to wake them up, but in vain. Perhaps they simply don't hear."

I can only counter with the assertion that all war dead suffer the same fate of being quickly forgotten. Statistics are what endure the longest: so many hundreds of thousands in the first, so many in the second world war. And I conclude my argument by saying:

"There are those that remember them, all the same, either out of spiritual kinship or for the sake of an argument, for patriotic reasons, or purely egotistical ones. You know that, old Giovannino, because you wrote in your diary: 'On my calendar I mark every passing day with a cross. After the war is over some men will be decorated with shiny medals, while others will have nothing to pin on their worn jackets but the penciled crosses symbolic of their dead days.' "

But my ragged friend still shakes his head.

"I must go now," he says. "That little Albertino who used to keep you company in the *Lager* is waiting for me."

"And where do you stay?" I ask him.

"Oh, in one place and another. Don't worry; if ever you need us, we'll be there. *Aufwiedersehen,* Giovannino."

Albertino returns, with a fair number of pictures

taken. I point to the fourth cross at the left-hand side of
the second row and tell him to photograph it.

"Who's there?" he asks.

"Just one like all the rest. *Unbekannt Ausland Soldat.*"

The *Lager* of Wietzendorf is in running order, too,
inhabited by refugees or some other species of the same
kind, but the same oppressively gloomy air pervades it.
Even with TV antennas on the roofs, the stucco barracks still recall to me the dens of filth with icicles hanging from the ceilings and rats running over our faces. I
can see a hole in the ground, which used to be a place
of solitary confinement.

Albertino is asking for all sorts of details, but I make
no reply. Everything has been engulfed by the hole,
and buried. What use is there in digging up and bringing to light a collection of sordid memories? The first
prerequisite for citizenship in the new United Europe is
a joyful ability to forget.

5. Miss Germany, Good-Bye!

The distance from Wietzendorf to Bergen is eight miles.
Slowly I drive over the road which I formerly covered
on foot, with a knapsack full of rags slung over my shoulder, amid a crowd of ragged men. We left Wietzendorf
at seven o'clock in the morning of April 22, 1945. The

situation was highly complex, because although the English had encircled the Germans and one of their patrols had penetrated the German lines and set us free, we, in our turn, had Germans all around us.

The Germans had set up a battery of mortars on the north side of the camp, just outside the barbed-wire fence, in order to shoot at the English position to the south, a *katrinka* on the west side to strike at the English on the east, and a second battery of mortars plus a second *katrinka* on the east, for what purpose God only knows.

In other words, showers of German cannon shots and grenades went over our heads, while the English were not able to focus their aim and counter this attack for fear of hitting the four thousand French officers lodged within the *Lager*. The French officers were under the protection of the International Red Cross, and because the Germans, at this desperate moment, did not want to get into further trouble, they decided to disband the camp and let the internees go over to the English lines. We Italians enjoyed no Red Cross protection, and so there was no particular reason why we should go free, but we trailed after the French, and when the English saw us coming they did not send us back. (It must be admitted that even if the International Red Cross never moved a finger in our behalf, another relief organization did do something for us. When we were suffering cold, hunger and fleas in the camp of Beniaminovo in Poland, we received envelopes full of extremely useful phonograph needles.)

The English didn't make any fuss. For one thing, there were Americans on the spot, ready to load our baggage on their trucks. And eventually, we were transformed from German prisoners into English ones. But not until after the incredible between-the-acts story of Bergen.

I have told the story of Bergen before, and no variation can improve upon it. Just let my readers imagine the state of mind of men who for nineteen months had endured filth, hunger and melancholy, when they found themselves free, with a prosperous town served up to them on a silver platter. And how they carried on in the spotless houses and neatly trimmed gardens, where a buried treasure of flour, butter, bacon and tinned meat awaited discovery. Then, to add to the confusion, were the hordes of freed Russian prisoners who were beating the area, stealing everything they could carry and smashing what they could not steal.

As we drive very slowly toward Bergen, Albertino listens angrily to my story.

"Poor Germans!" he exclaims. "Just think how we should have felt if, while you were a prisoner, a horde of escapees had burst in upon us and thrown grandmother, grandfather, mother, Carlotta and me out of our own house!"

According to him, I ought to have gone straight to the English commander at Bergen and said: "No sir, I'll sleep on a wooden bench if necessary, but the comfortable bed and the 1,200 pounds of sugar found in the grocer's house where my comrades and I are billetted must remain untouched. The grocer and his family weren't the ones to throw me into a filthy *Lager*. The German people aren't really to blame. It was just the fortunes of war." This is the way Albertino thinks I should have behaved. In theory, I agree, and I re-enter Bergen with shame upon my head. I remember the name of a "Hotel Hartung," but we find it in the process of rebuilding and alteration.

"You must have left it in a pretty mess, if it's taken them twelve years to make repairs," is Albertino's comment.

We take a couple of rooms in another place, and as soon as we have set down our luggage, I go out to take a look at the town. The first thing I search for is the combined house and store of the grocer. There it is, quite plain to see. The shop window has been modernized, but the building is just the same as before. I go in, with the excuse of buying a bottle of brandy, and am met at the door by the fragrant odor of spices. Because I don't wish to make myself conspicuous, I say to Albertino:

"I'm going back to the hotel. See if you can get a good picture. The room where I slept is on the ground floor."

I spend the rest of the afternoon in my hotel room, looking out of my window at the Germany I once knew.

After we have had supper and written the usual number of postcards, I suggest that we go for a stroll together. Albertino says that he has other ideas in mind. Finally I get him to define them. It seems that in one of

the downstairs rooms of the hotel, there is going to be
a dance, and he wants to look in on it. And so, instead
of going for a walk, I sit down with him at a table in
the "ball-room." It's not the most thrilling way to spend
the evening, from my point of view, to watch a small-
town dance and listen to the music of a three-piece
band, accordion, violin and cello. But my son is seven-
teen years old and has the exact same tastes that I had
at his age. He'd be ready to dance even if his leg were
encased in plaster. At first he doesn't admit it, but
eventually he murmurs:

"I wouldn't mind having a turn around the room."

"We're in a foreign country, remember, and this is a
very small town. You know for yourself how narrow
people can be in such a place."

He does know, and from sad experience. One afternoon last summer, he got me to let him go over to the
town next to ours, where he had heard there was going
to be good music and dancing. He came home feeling
very hurt, because no girl would dance with a "stranger." When I was a boy, things were even worse. If an
"out-of-towner" asked a girl for a dance, he either got
told then and there to go to bed, or else the local boys
lay in wait for him after the dance and roughed him up
in a way he wasn't likely to forget. Now he hesitates for
a moment and then screws up his courage.

"I may as well try. If I get no for an answer, it's not
so terribly important."

There he's dead wrong! International relations often
hinge on just such apparently unimportant trifles. I

came to Germany with the best of intentions, and so far I've looked at it with a sympathetic eye. But if that nitwit girl toward whom my son is making his way refuses to dance with him, then Germany will have me for an enemy again, and one without pity! I may be able to forgive Germany for having detained me nineteen months in an internment camp, but I could never forgive a daughter of Germany for turning down my son!

Historical moments go by, as Albertino makes a polite, schoolboy bow. Germany's fate hangs on a thread. Thank heaven, the girl is no nitwit, but a charming and civilized young lady.

All my resentments are forgotten. I have put behind me the statement of a German newspaper reporter: "Italians are good drivers, but very poor fighting men," and the one made by a stuffed-shirt individual at Hannover: "England, the United States, France, Germany, Switzerland, all these nations have a policy of some kind. But no one ever hears of an Italian policy." By which he must have meant that, politically speaking, Italy doesn't really matter. No, bygones are bygones. Albertino is dancing with Miss Germany, while I drink to a United Europe.

Even in this small-town hotel, there is someone that recognizes my handlebar mustache. In my honor the band strikes up *Guaglione,* which in German is called *Peppino* and talks about a "Peppone," whose name rhymes with *"balcone."* Some of the people around know a few words of Italian; they sit down at my table and ask for autographs. Among them there are boys the same age as Albertino.

"Who knows?" I think to myself. "I may have seen that boy there, all smiles, twelve years ago, in a wagon where his mother had stored all her earthly goods before she left bombarded Berlin to seek safety in some country haystack."

Because I remember clearly the long line of silent, bombed-out evacuees, the women with stony, impenetrable faces. Perhaps the girl who is dancing with my son, too, was among them. Someone asks if this is my first trip to Germany, and I answer: "Yes, the first."